CHYNA

Using Reiki

Practical Essays that Bring Reiki
into Daily Practice

Copyright © 2020 by Chyna Honey

All rights reserved. This book or any portion thereof may not be reproduced or used in any manner whatsoever without the express written permission of the publisher except for the use of brief quotations in a book review.

Printed in the United States of America

First Printing, 2020

ISBN 978-0-578-79897-4

Library of Congress Control Number: 2020921971

Conversations included in this book have been set down to the best of the author's ability, although names and some of the details have been changed to protect the privacy of individuals.

Cover and Interior Layout Design by: InsomniaARS
Author Photo: Deborah Tarrant

Published by: Piper Peony Publishing in San Francisco, California
https://chynahoney.com

*For everyone who has received a
Reiki attunement.*

Table of Contents

PREFACE

PART I — ESTABLISHING VALUE

Introduction ------------------------------- 4
What is Reiki? ----------------------------- 7
What Reiki Does and What It Doesn't Do -------- 15
Why Reiki is a Critical Part of Self-Care ---------- 21
Using Reiki Will Improve Overall Self-Care ------- 27
Closing Thoughts --------------------------- 32

PART II — IN PRACTICE

Introduction ------------------------------- 36
Coming-to-Terms: Working Through Internal
Inhibitors of Practice ----------------------- 39
The Cupped Hand Position ------------------- 47
Working Through the External Factors that Appear
to Impede Practice ------------------------- 57
How Convenience Can Impede Practice --------- 67
A Brief Review ----------------------------- 71
Closing Thoughts --------------------------- 74

PART III — ANSWERING FOLLOW-UP QUESTIONS

Introduction — 78
How Do I Become More Comfortable with Reiki? — 83
Why Don't I Feel my Reiki Anymore, or Why is it Less Intense? — 91
If I Don't Feel Reiki, How Do I Know That It's Working? — 97
Why Didn't Reiki Alleviate All My Symptoms? — 103
Do I Lose Reiki if I Fail to Use It? — 107
Understanding the Attunement Levels of Reiki — 109
Closing Thoughts — 116

PART IV — UNDERSTANDING DIFFERENCES

Introduction — 120
Understanding the Differences Between Acupuncture and Reiki — 123
Differences between Meditation and Reiki — 129
The Differences Between Craniosacral Therapy (CST) and Reiki — 135
The Differences Between Massage and Reiki — 139
Closing Thoughts — 143

AUTHOR'S FINAL NOTE
THANK YOU
ABOUT THE AUTHOR

Preface

Reiki is a beloved practice, and this book is in many ways a series of love letters. These love letters are more instructional and focused than romantic or sentimental, but each conveys a passion for helping students turn their sought-after instruction into a self-sustaining daily practice.

The truth is, most students who become attuned to Reiki won't establish the daily habit of practice, despite the fact that most will come in with excitement to learn and leave feeling alive and wonderful. So, what's missing, then, and how can I help students turn a wonderful, life-changing experience into daily practice?

That question is the driving force behind this book. This series of love letters, which going forward I'll call essays, are written with the singular goal of helping students go beyond the wonder they first feel with Reiki and into the commitment of daily practice without losing the joy. Six years ago, I wrote *Understanding Reiki: From Self-Care to Energy Medicine* because I found that while there was no shortage of people who had a Reiki attunement, there were very few who practiced regularly, if they practiced at all. At the time, my conclusion to this dilemma was that people don't use what they don't understand, even if the class they went to was amazing, uplifting and even life-changing.

Looking at the problem, I came to see that understanding precedes practice because we value what we understand, and we use what we value. I found this to be true time and time again, but in the years that followed, what also became clear was that understanding alone simply wasn't enough. Students also need and benefit from a steady stream of encouragement. Encouragement that reminds them why they came to Reiki in the first place, and why they love how it makes them feel. Encouragement that explicitly reminds them why they need to practice. I wrote this book then to offer that steady stream of encouragement.

I do this by methodically exploring why Reiki is valuable, providing supplemental instruction on how to practice, answering frequently asked follow-up questions and then explaining in detail how Reiki differs from but complements other popular natural healing practices. In short, this book picks up where the last one left off.

My enduring hope for this book is that it provides clear, nuanced answers about Reiki. I hope that you finish it feeling enriched, better prepared and more confident in your practice. I hope that you find it easy to read, to enjoy and to share with others, but most of all, more than anything else, I hope it encourages you to practice every day.

PART I

Establishing Value

Introduction

Having value in something is to regard it as useful or beneficial. For the most part, our values will guide our decisions and determine our actions. Our values will inspire the work we do and motivate us to pursue certain relationships. They are essential in helping us to commit to new habits. You see, it's not enough to know something is good for you, or bad for you, as the case may be. That is just information, and people discard information all the time. It's harder to ignore something we value. So, if you want to start a new habit, firmly establish value for that new habit, then allow your newly established value to do what values do: lead. Because when value leads, practice follows, and before you know it, your positive habit is formed. This then proves your newly established value to be truly valuable. In time, your confidence in practice will grow, making the habit a positive life change that is both easily sustainable and enjoyable. It's a neat cycle that goes from desire for the positive change to the fulfillment of daily practice. That is our aim with Reiki.

In an effort to provide greater context for this, consider another everyday example of how our values lead us into action, our practice of daily dental hygiene. Now, it's hard to say that everyone enjoys the practice, but it's easy to state that most of us have been taught to value it. Those values have been reinforced with personal experience that show us that daily practice helps us keep small problems, like the need to remove daily sugars from our teeth, small. As a result, we all know that brushing our teeth is good for us, but that knowledge alone is not what drives to brush each day — so what does? Certainly, knowing the benefit is a plus, but most of us brush as often as we do because we value the appearance of a bright smile, we value the smell of clean breath and we view both as a marker for good health and a requirement for a professional and/or attractive appearance. Our values are based more on feeling, not thinking. As a result, we are motivated more by how having good dental hygiene make us feel than being told the benefits of fluoride. Our mouth feels cleaner, our breath smells fresher, and this helps us feel more comfortable in close spaces. Our smile appears brighter, and this helps us to feel more confident in our appearance. These feelings support the values we were given for daily dental hygiene, and because this value that was passed on to us in youth has been consistently practiced, it became a daily habit that improved our appearance and our oral well-being, so there is little conflict or question about whether it's a practice worthy of your time.

So, when it comes to establishing value for Reiki, I recommend mirroring a similar model, which requires more than an explanation on what Reiki is. It also requires context that helps students take that explanation and make it immediately applicable to their lives. When this is followed by an opportunity for practice, students can use their direct experience to feel firsthand why a daily Reiki practice is worthy of their time.

Now, that may seem pretty straightforward, but for the information to really take hold, most people will need to hear it repeated on multiple occasions over time. They will also need to have that information accompanied by practice, which is why I direct my students to self-administer Reiki whenever I teach. The two, instruction and practice, are a winning combination that both facilitates effective learning and reinforces the value that a daily practice will bring to your well-being. To that end, Part I has two main objectives: to explain what Reiki is, and to explain why Reiki is so valuable.

*The question
that is the prelude
to practice.*

What is Reiki?

A helpful approach to answering the question, "What is Reiki?" is to begin by clarifying that Reiki is the name given to two separate but interrelated things. First, Reiki is the name given to a natural healing vibration. Second, Reiki is the name given to the formalized healing system that teaches students how to use this vibration. The word is used interchangeably; however, it's fair to say that when most people speak about Reiki, they are referring to the formalized healing system. In an effort to help students understand Reiki, I will review both before moving into using the terms as it relates to practice in Part II.

Reiki, the healing vibration, is comparable to the vibration of sound but considerably subtler. While this vibration is of use to humans and can be channeled by students who have been attuned to it, the vibration itself is not a human creation. The same can be said of sound. While humans can make sound, use sound, and benefit from sound, sound itself is not a human creation. We may enjoy and benefit from the use of Reiki and sound and many other vibrations available to us within our shared environment, but it exists independent of us. The value inherent in knowing this is humility. It reminds us that there are things in this world that exist independent of us.

In contrast to the vibration, Reiki, the formalized healing system that teaches students how to use the vibration, is a human creation. It was designed to teach others how to use the vibration for the purpose of healing. This places Reiki, the formalized healing system, under our domain, and subjects it to spheres of influence that over time and across cultures have had the unintended consequence of altering the way Reiki is taught and understood today. As a human creation, this has been unavoidable, and the truth is, trying to learn about natural healing has long been considered tricky business. This is because vague language tends to permeate its teachings, leaving many students to rely on faith or to fill in the blanks when a clear, relatable understanding appears unavailable. This is made all the more challenging when you consider that Reiki is learned through the body, not only the mind, and most of us have become accustomed to learning through the mind, not the body. Still, even as we learn through the body, to learn completely and effectively, we need to take our mind with us when learning Reiki. This means we need to help the mind make sense of what the body is experiencing, or in time the mind will reject what the body learned. To teach the mind, we provide clear explanation. To teach the body, we practice Reiki. To make the most of both, we do those things together. To that end, if you aren't already, this is the point where I ask you to give yourself Reiki as you read along.

Living life on Planet Earth, we are consistently affected by all sorts of things, from subtle energies to things that are more material in nature, such as tree sap, bird poop, and wind. The effect these things have on us results in what is best described as "wear and tear." It's the price we pay for living in a shared environment. In this sense, the wear and tear we experience is not unlike the wear and tear we experience in our homes and our cars. Wear and tear is the result of use — daily, unencumbered use — not destructive forces. This wear and tear sounds expected, and it is, and for the most part, it's benign. To ensure that we do our part to keep small imbalances small, we thankfully have a slew of practices at our disposal to help us take care of and remedy it. We all know that our possessions' appearances are improved when they are properly cared for, and that their longevity is determined more by the daily care given to those items than by the big repairs needed when our attention to their maintenance wanes. The same is true for our body and well-being. Our need to remedy daily wear and tear has existed as long as we have, but for the most part, we have limited this remedy to applying it to physical issues because that is what we've been taught. We wash our face, brush our teeth and clean our ears. But now, with Reiki, we are extending our remedy and applying it to more subtle forms of wear and tear: the wear and tear that is the result of subtle energies in our shared space that we often experience as real consequences.

This type of wear and tear is most often experienced as tension. I feel like I should say that again: *this type of wear and tear is most often experienced as tension.* Tension inhibits our ability to relax naturally, so we feel less comfortable in our own skin. This impediment to relaxation starts us on a slippery slope, and before we know it, we feel imbalanced and out of sorts. Our body feels tense, and our motivations turn away from seeking enjoyment to needing distraction. This is often accompanied by negative side effects or symptoms, such as a deterioration of our sleep patterns or the quality of our diet and overall hydration. Meaning: we will feel less well. Our well-being is slowly becoming more and more compromised. But because it's a matter of wear and tear, we either don't see its decline or we don't know how to fix it, and before you know it, this lowered well-being is just how you feel, and it becomes the new normal.

That is, until we can blame it on age. We've all learned how to dismiss wear and tear as just the way things are. That sense of helplessness often drives students to seek something, anything that can help, and so they soon find themselves attending a Reiki class. It's a knowing that defies explanation. The student may not even be consciously aware of it, but still there's a knowing that life doesn't have to be this way — at least not always. This knowing that's hard to describe is that, when used, Reiki provides remedy and repair to the parts of us most affected by general wear and tear. That is worth repeating. *When used, Reiki provides remedy and repair to the parts of us most affected by general wear and tear.*

For this reason, I can't tell you how wonderful it is to teach level 1 students. To see their eyes light up as I explain Reiki and as I talk about this knowing that brought them to class, I see students actually sit up and drawn themselves closer into the discussion. Later in the class when I explain the need for the attunement, excitement fills their eyes to the point where they look like they can't wait for it to begin. In a word, it's wonderful, so here I take a moment to review why we need an attunement in the first place. What follows is an excerpt from my first book, *Understanding Reiki: From Self-Care to Energy Medicine.*

To practice Reiki, you will first need a Reiki attunement. A Reiki attunement is a short energetic ceremony that gently returns your system to a more natural state, and that more natural state makes you a natural channel for the Reiki vibration to flow through. Over time, because of our own evolution — most notably, the overuse of the mind, our energy system has become kinked, in a manner of speaking, not unlike a hose. When a hose is kinked, water flows through, but in drips and drabs, and the amount of water that comes through it is not enough for what is needed. To get more water, you straighten the hose, and water flows through unimpeded and smoothly. A Reiki attunement is the energy equivalent of straightening the hose. It's a natural adjustment made during a brief ceremony by a Reiki teacher for their student.

> *Without an attunement, the channel remains kinked. To be clear, it's not that some are kinked and others aren't. Everyone's kinked until they have received an attunement. An attunement is a part of the Reiki class, and before you go in for an attunement, your teacher will provide you with instruction and expectations for it, so I will avoid those details here except to say that receiving an attunement is a wonderful experience and will leave you feeling amazing.*

To be clear, Reiki isn't the answer for all that ails or creates stress, but it's the answer and remedy for the wear and tear we incur and experience on a daily basis.

So, when I'm asked what Reiki is, I start by first differentiating between the vibration and the healing system. Then, I build upon that by stating that Reiki is a healing system that promotes well-being through daily practice. Finally, I get into detail by explaining that Reiki provides remedy and repair to daily wear and tear. To be clear, in all those explanations, I use the word Reiki to describe the vibration in the first part only — everything after that refers to the formalized healing system that utilizes that vibration.

This classifies Reiki as both a restorative and a preventative healing practice. However, because of its nature and because of ours, Reiki often fails to receive the full credit it is due, and generally this is for two reasons. The first is because most explanations of Reiki fall short of providing a clear or a complete explanation of Reiki. So, the concept remains vague or intangible, and when it is either of those things, it's undervalued at best or not valued at worst. The second is that the impact of Reiki will often feel more like a whisper than sound like a bang. Meaning that unless you're paying close attention, you will rarely know what imbalances Reiki has remedied, or what that remedy has saved you from in terms of ailments, illnesses or discomforts. Additionally, the reveals of Reiki tend to come more in small but significant changes than big a-ha moments. This point is worthy of reverence, not dismissal; but to be fair, many will prefer a more dramatic sort of change to the gentler, sublime one. If dramatic change is more your speed, I assure you, change will be made, so stay with it and practice. It may seem more like a gentle knock than a bang, but if you listen and pay attention to your bodily needs, you'll hear it. And while you will never really know what Reiki has saved you from, you can know how you feel after practice, and you can know how you feel in general because you made the time to practice. By the way, this is also true of tooth-brushing. You practice that every day, and you'll never know what it's saved you from, but you know how your mouth feels when you do. Spoiler alert: the most common feeling following Reiki practice is relaxation, and I know we can all use more of that feeling.

With that, I'll end with the story of one of my clients who soon became a student. Her name was Anna. Anna was a client who came in every two weeks for Reiki and she loved her sessions. She never missed an appointment and often came in excited and left relieved. One day after a session, I mentioned to her that I had a Level-1 course coming up and invited her to be a part of it. I told her she could learn how to do Reiki, and if she wanted to, she could do it for herself.

She got nervous at first. She thought I was suggesting she stop coming in for sessions and start treating herself at home.

I wasn't saying that, although I told her it would be an option. Instead, I assured her that I was inviting her to learn why she enjoyed Reiki so much and found healing appointments so valuable.

Her nervousness turned to disinterest. She said, "I don't care what it is. I only care that I get it and it makes me feel better."

I said, "Fair enough. Receiving it is more valuable than knowing what it is or even why it helps you feel better."

Then she got curious and asked, "Would it help me to know more about Reiki?"

I said, "Only if you're interested, but given the way you talk about loving our sessions, I think you'd love it."

In the end she decided to attend, and she was so glad she did. Her enthusiasm for her sessions became exuberance for her practice. She still came in for the occasional session, and she was even brighter when she did.

She said, "I didn't realize how much I would enjoy learning the explanation that describes my experiences."

To this day, Anna is one of my most dedicated students.

> *Knowing what something does is incomplete if you don't know what it doesn't do.*

What Reiki Does and What it Doesn't Do

It's important when seeking to understand Reiki, and natural healing as a whole, to understand which healing practices are best served to treat symptoms that are caused by issues such as wear and tear, trauma, injury, illness and/or karma. Generally speaking, these five are gross classifications of the type of issues a person would see a healer for. Reiki is a healing practice that provides remedy and repair to daily wear and tear. That's it. Reiki is not an effective treatment for trauma, nor does it provide effective repair to injury. It does not provide remedy to illness or help one resolve issues associated with karma. Understanding this helps us to distinguish between the minor but consistent daily effects we all experience as a result of wear and tear from the notable, immediate and destructive impact experienced as a result of any of the other groupings.

As a course of daily life, we are bombarded with energies that stress our energy system and ultimately our body, mind and emotional state. I realize the word *bombarded* can infer a form of aggressiveness, and I'm not using it to describe a sort of assault of the energy or of the senses. Instead, I use the word to infer a relentlessness of interfacing with energies that coexist in our shared environment. Whether we are aware of those energies or not, we are affected by the relentlessness of them. Reiki helps us to heal from near-imperceptible effects that are the result of this bombardment of energies. As a way to name or classify this type of daily occurrence, I refer to it as daily wear and tear.

To be clear, daily wear and tear is not trauma. It is not injury or illness, although both injury and illness can occur as the result of long-term, unresolved and uncared for wear and tear. Think here of a house. If small repairs are not made and daily care is not given, over time, significant repairs will be required and the house itself may start to fall apart. When this happens, the care given to remedy general wear and tear will not be enough to fix what's broken. Consider a minor leak in the roof. If not tended to and repaired, that leak can create lasting damage and even threaten the integrity of the roof over time. If that happens, a small repair will no longer be enough to fix the roof, making a replacement of the roof or a significantly costly repair necessary. But when wear and tear is tended to with care, the house will have greater longevity, be easier and less costly to maintain and will be a more enjoyable host to its tenant.

Reiki is the remedy to general wear and tear, and it works without fail every time to do just that. If you have symptoms as the result of trauma, Reiki will not remedy those symptoms. It may make the intensity of certain symptoms lessen, but that should not be confused with Reiki being curative for symptoms related to trauma. In a case like that, what Reiki has done is provide remedy to the wear and tear that made the traumatic symptom louder, and therefore more noticeable. With remedy provided to wear and tear, the symptoms caused by trauma are no longer compounded by the wear and tear, and so those symptoms can appear quieter. An example of this would be anxiety. To be sure, there are cases where Reiki can alleviate low-level feelings of anxiety, but only if that anxiety is the result of daily wear and tear. If that anxiety is the result of trauma, Reiki may help to take the edge off because it's providing remedy to the added anxiety caused by wear and tear that's making the underlying anxiety caused by trauma louder. But, to be clear, Reiki doesn't provide remedy to the anxiety caused by the trauma. For that, something else, something additional, is needed — not something in place of Reiki, something to complement it. Because the need for the daily healing that Reiki provides will never cease. Here I've used trauma as the example, but the same is true for illness, injury or issues associated with karma. These ailments or symptoms require different forms of healing.

Sonni was a client of mine who was the Reiki student of one of my teachers. She once told me in session that she was using her Reiki to keep her from getting the flu and that she felt let down by Reiki when she eventually came down with it. Even though she wasn't taught that Reiki would keep her from getting sick, she still thought it would, or so she had hoped.

I understand. We all want to feel we have more control than we do, especially when it comes to our health. The problem is that we are all often distracted by imagining we can control something we can't, and when we do, it's often at the expense of abdicating control over the things that we can. I gently told Sonni that Reiki could not keep her from getting the flu or cure her from it. It will likely minimize the discomfort of the flu, not because it's directly affecting the flu virus but because it is providing repair and remedy to daily wear and tear that, if left unchecked, could make her symptoms of flu more uncomfortable. I also tried to assure her that her coming down with the flu was not a sign of failure. Instead, it was a sign that she lives a full life and that she likely interacts with other people throughout the day. And as it turns out, Sonni is a schoolteacher. This conversation helped to put Sonni at ease and helped to provide some context for what Reiki does do and for what it doesn't do.

As this book is being completed in the age of Covid-19, I've received questions about whether Reiki can help protect someone from the virus. The answer is no, absolutely not. Reiki is not an immune booster, at least not directly. Again, clarity on this provides context for understanding the role Reiki has in your overall wellness. Reiki is not an immune booster; it does not work on the immune system. What Reiki does is provide remedy and repair from daily wear and tear, and if you have significant daily wear and tear and you start using Reiki every day, you will start to feel better. That may feel like a real energy boost — in fact, for most it does. However, that's not the same as an immune booster. As illustrated in the above story, Reiki can't protect anyone from a virus. Covid-19 is an infectious disease and as such, Reiki cannot provide remedy for it or protect someone from getting it.

Still, Reiki works, and it works all the time. And the value in understanding what it does and what it doesn't do is twofold. First, it empowers its users to make better choices and provide necessary remedies when symptoms due to wear and tear are present. To be sure, you will not always know what is generating a symptom, but with a daily Reiki practice, you will at least have one cause of symptoms you can eliminate, which is wear and tear. Second, because there is a good amount of vague language that's used when discussing Reiki, many people have come to believe that Reiki is meant to do things it's not. This often generates disappointment when Reiki is believed to have failed or come up short. It also tends to put people off from Reiki and raises questions about its credibility. For these reasons, I find it's important not only to discuss what Reiki does but what it doesn't do, so that its purpose can be understood and the expectations of its users can be properly met.

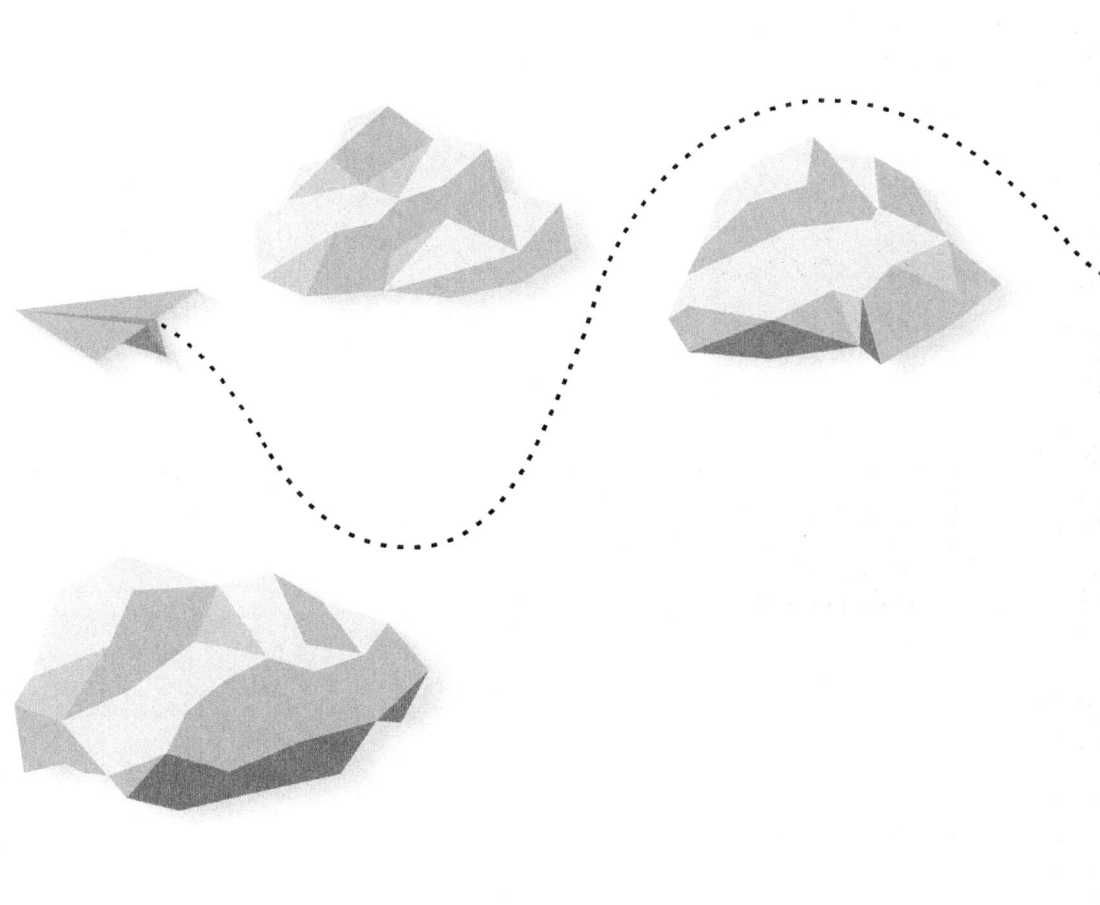

> *Taking care of our energetic needs makes it easier to take care of our physical ones.*

Why Reiki is a Critical Part of our Self-Care

As above, so below, is a principle used in helping to explain a great manner of things. Generally, it refers to the idea that the microcosm reflects the macrocosm, the inner reflects the outer, the individual reflects society. I use this principle in explaining why Reiki is a critical part of our self-care regimen, for it quite aptly points to something that intrinsically we already know: that our subtle nature reflects our physical nature. How we feel on the inside is often reflected back to us on the outside. We also know from direct experience that when we take care of small problems, we have fewer big problems. When we regularly brush and floss, we have better breath and fewer cavities. When we get enough sleep, it's easier to think and be creative. When we eat nourishing foods, we are stronger, and when we stay adequately hydrated, it's easier to focus, defecate, sleep and even move. All these things fall under self-care, and each provide an example of care given for and by the self for the purpose of providing repair and remedy to the general wear and tear of daily life, also known as use and being.

To be sure, we come into the world with a significant list of self-care requirements. It's the price we pay for living. Rightfully so, the self-care required by our body is what we focus on most, and for our body we need to eat, sleep, drink, breathe, move and clean, among other things. But our energy has self-care requirements as well, and while we aren't taught about those in childhood, they do have a significant impact on the quality of our well-being. A Reiki attunement and class enables a person to meet one of those self-care requirements, and in meeting that one, others are made easier to do.

Energetically speaking, every one of us is affected by the energies that exist in our shared environment. It's impossible to avoid – a bit like the weather. You can try to shield yourself from it and have some temporary success, but you're still a part of the world that is forever influenced and at the mercy of the weather. These shared energies are not going anywhere, they are here just as we are, and for time immemorial, we have lived together in our shared environments. However, today, just as there are more humans, there are more energies, and the way these energies affect us, is energy wear and tear. Energy wear and tear is most commonly experienced as tension. Subtle tensions develop into bodily tension, and then our mind tries to provide us with reasons why we feel tense. The downside to that, however, is our mind's explanations often have us feeling worse, not better, and can start to turn our bodily tension into mental stress. This then starts to loop back into the body, and the whole system is made all the worse for the wear. That is because the general wear and tear we experience each day is now being compounded by mental projections meant to explain tension that really started off as no more than a sort of energetic debris you were hit with throughout the day.

To say that in a different way, because our minds don't know about energetic wear and tear but need to find an explanation for the tension we feel, it starts to run through the events of the day or go back into the files of past events or fears of future events to try to explain why the body feel tense. This process transforms tension into stress, and that stress and the fears it generates tend to make the body even more tense. So, in the absence of daily practice, our tension can become stress, our stress brings about more tension and our imbalances can become symptoms that affect the freedom and ease we feel when we are well. When that happens, we can rather quickly find ourselves on a slippery slope of diminishing self-care maintenance. Before we know it, we start to drink less water, becoming dehydrated. We also may start to eat less, while others may start eating more, but neither are likely to eat nutritiously. We start to sleep less, bolstering our need to drink more coffee and we stop exercising or we start to over-exercise. The system as a whole begins to feel compromised, we feel out of sorts, and all that is left is to reverse course or double down. My eternal hope is that when you find yourself in this or a similar scenario that you always reverse course, because the good news is, we can start again. Reiki is the remedy to energy wear and tear and is an effective first step on the journey back.

Understanding this is part of accepting that everything starts as energy and is made manifest into the physical. The energy aspect of us is our "as above," the physical aspect is our "so below." To that end, in terms of our self-care practices, Reiki is our "as above," and things like eating, drinking, sleeping, even washing our face, our "so below." So, when the energetic aspects of our experience are cared for, it becomes easier to care for the physical, emotional and mental ones. That's not to suggest that Reiki makes the sometimes-difficult task of self-care easy, but it does make doing them easier because, at least energetically speaking, there's less static in the way.

Dinesh was a level-1 student who asked to take a level 2 in an attempt to pick his practice back up. Dinesh owned a small business that not only required a lot of time and attention but required him to travel as well. With so much going on, he found himself forgetting to practice. Days of missed practice turned to weeks and before he knew it, he wasn't sleeping well. He loved his tea but was afraid to drink more of it throughout the day out of fear it would make it even harder to sleep. Instead, he knew Reiki was the answer but also knew he needed the reminders and the support to get back into practice. Dinesh left his level-2 attunement class a new man. Revigorated after just two days of practice, he vowed never to fall off the wagon again.

I replied, "Never is a long time, and perhaps it's not a fair commitment to make. Life is full and has many demands, and those demands might gnaw at your commitment sometimes. And that's okay, because you can always return to practice, just as you have now. So, enjoy what you have and know that I am here, as is your community, and that we are all made better by support and gentle reminders that beacon us back to practice."

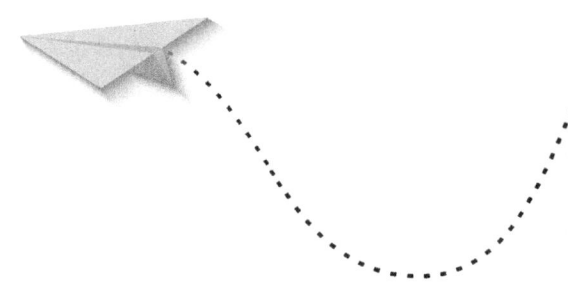

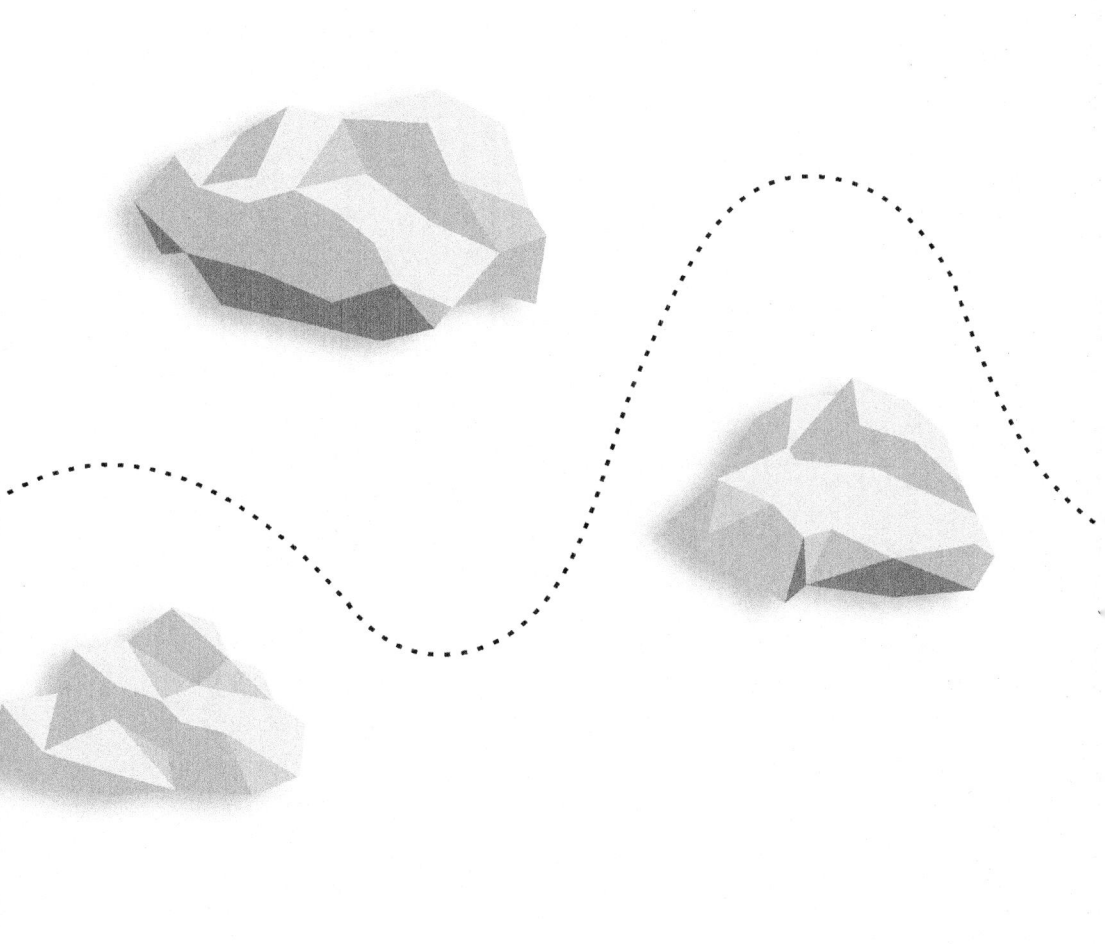

> *By understanding what it means to be well, it's easier to take responsibility for those necessary daily tasks.*

Using Reiki Will Improve Overall Self-Care

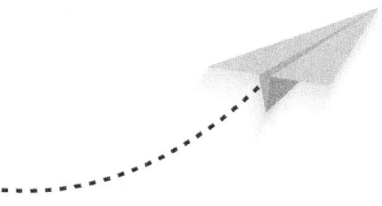

On a daily basis, our attention and responsibilities are often pulled in many different directions. When times get tough and our stress levels increase, our perception of time and how much we have of it diminishes. This is often when our self-care practice becomes sacrificed under the guise that giving ourselves less enables us to give others more. It's not that we don't know the opposite is true, we do, but despite that we still have a hard time accepting it to the point of putting it into practice, and that is because we have a value problem. Society teaches us to value selfless acts over acts of self-care. In fact, acts of self-care are often judged by others as selfish. So even though we know what we should do, instead, we do what we have been taught to value.

Still, we want to help others and we believe ourselves to have something to give. We also want to believe that we can do it all, and if we can't, then we want to believe we are robust enough to pay the price for it later. Always later, and despite our learning time and time again that when we stop meeting our basic self-care needs, we deplete the source of support we have to offer others, our tendency is to persist in this bad habit. Eventually we start to feel frayed around the edges, or at the very least, things we try to accomplish become harder. We try our best to change it, to do better next time, and in some measure, we succeed. But still, most of us will, eventually, find ourselves back in the cycle.

But there is a way out and, you guessed it, it starts by reexamining and then starting to change what we value. We reorder our values to place our value for self-care just above our value for helping others, and we do that by accepting in our gut what we already know to be true. You give your best to others when you have already given your best to you. Give yourself things like good food, plenty of water, restful sleep, challenging activity and engaging work. I know that sounds like a tall order, but there is good news: Reiki is available, and using it will help. To be clear, while Reiki can't absolve us our prejudices or quiet our stubborn natures, Reiki does help us deepen the well from which we give, and in so doing, helps us gain greater awareness of our personal needs, which empowers us to improve all of our self-care practices.

It does this by providing the repair and remedy needed by the physical body and the aura that results from daily wear and tear. In short, it's the daily self-care your energy system needs to recover from its day. Even if you didn't do much, remember wear and tear isn't just defined as use; its definition includes being as well. Wear and tear is the price we pay for living in a body on this wonderful Planet Earth.

In addition to providing remedy and repair to daily wear and tear, Reiki provides the added, indirect benefit of helping to maintain, if not heighten, awareness of daily needs and providing the mental clarity and emotional balance to meet those needs. For example, after sustaining a strong daily practice of Reiki, a student will often report that her awareness of the daily hydration her body needs is greater than previously thought. In particular, she may notice that she's thirstier throughout the day and has an innate desire for more water, or she may notice that she's drinking more, and it's that change that informs her she's been long underhydrated. While at first, this may be an unwelcome annoyance with its increased number of trips to the bathroom, it's also a positive change that highlights an increased level of awareness regarding the body's relentless need for adequate daily hydration. Students who practice daily often make similar reports about sleep and diet. Ideally, a positive self-sustaining change in practice precedes the conscious awareness that things have changed, but regardless of the order, the increased self-awareness and the benefits it yields are a gift.

So then, how will you know Reiki is delivering on its promise to improve overall self-care? I've got some key markers for you to look for, but know that your habits may change before you're aware a change has occurred, and really, that's a great thing. Buying a new water bottle or bringing that one you bought some time ago out of the cupboard without any conflict or sense of obligation shows a significant improvement in your commitment to one of your body's basic needs. The awareness that you're tired so you start off to bed, despite the older habit to binge one more episode, is a real sign that your priorities have changed for the better. That change in priorities signals a shift away from the distraction of what ails, to care for what is needed to help nurture wellness. These small but significant changes are the everyday ah-ha moments that are often missed due to the wear and tear we feel, leaving us to wait for the louder uh-oh moments to pierce through the static. Loosely translated, small but significant changes amount to a greater general sense of ease. A gentle self-check-in each day, or each week, can help provide insight. Overall, what you're looking for is a feeling of "that's better," and better in more things. This can include better sleep, better hydration, less tired, fewer headaches, feeling more emotionally balanced throughout the day, finding it easier to eat better and feeling more relaxed. If you're prone to headaches, you may notice a change there, or if you tend to drink multiple cups of coffee a day, you may notice that subtly, the number of cups consumed has decreased. These may seem small but are significant changes.

If, however, you want a specific goal to aim for seeing in your Reiki results, I suggest starting with a gentle attention given to thirst over the next couple of weeks. Generally speaking, this is where students feel it most. It should not be a distracting feeling or a swell of thirst that comes out of nowhere, instead it's more of a steady, persistent need, making it easier to accommodate. Once you've got that, turn your attention to sleep, and gently notice if there are any changes in the quality of sleep or a new need for more rest. The latter might seem worrying at first, but it's not the feeling that's new, it's your awareness to the feeling that is. And the remedy for that is simply more rest.

This reminds me of a student named Jaye who just before a level-2 review class was talking with her classmates about a new water bottle she bought. Another student had just complimented it, and she was thrilled to share how she had just started using it and how much better she felt because she was drinking more. At the time, she didn't connect this with her Reiki practice, and I didn't say anything because class hadn't started yet.

But as we got into class, Jaye said she noticed that she needed more rest recently and wondered if Reiki was somehow making her tired. It wasn't, and I was excited by the question because it presented a great introduction into the topic of self-care. I also knew this opening would help me to circle back on her earlier statements about her new water bottle. I assured her that Reiki was not making her tired. I explained that Reiki didn't expend energy, it helped fortify it. We don't lose energy when we practice, we strengthen it by tending to the minor, everyday wear and tear we experience each day. To prove this, I encouraged the class to put it to the test. I asked the students to take a moment to practice. After a few minutes, I asked, "Is anyone tired?"

Jaye answered first. Jaye often answers first, and it's wonderful because in doing so, she gives other students the confidence to ask questions. Jaye said that she didn't feel tired, but she felt relaxed. I said, "Yes! And there's a difference between tired and relaxed, but most have a hard time telling the difference because people are so rarely truly relaxed. But that fact that she could tell the difference was not only brilliant, it was a testament to her practice. But that aside for a moment, it's not Reiki that makes you tired, but the improvement you've made to your energy self-care has helped you notice that you need more rest than you're currently getting." Then I really blew her mind when I said, "The same is true of your desire for more water throughout the day, and it was the celebration of that feeling that inspired the purchase of your new water bottle."

Jaye then sat back, beaming with satisfaction.

What is helpful to remember, from the student to the Master, is that Reiki starts as a self-care practice, and healing is a natural, daily activity. In fact, the necessity for advanced healing is often the result of a breakdown in a self-care practice. This breakdown or interruption of self-care is almost always preceded with the awareness that there isn't enough time or a self-negotiation that time will be made later and is only being temporarily sacrificed to help another or to complete a project at work, finish exams at school or for some other valued reason. And this serves as a key reminder that we all live in a world where more is expected of us than less, and when the going gets tough, we are usually the ones who deprive us most of the care we need. We alone have the power and the responsibility to change that. This is our constant; it's the nature of the world we are all a part of and have a part to play in. But given the chance, and with the opportunity taken, Reiki will help — it may even blow your mind.

Closing Thoughts

Everyone wants to feel better, enjoy greater health and the freedom it provides. In our darkest moments, it's our health and well-being we cling to most. In our brightest times, it's our vitality and vigor that inspires celebration. For the most part, how we feel determines how much we can do and how much we want to do. And while few discuss the health of their energy system, most will often refer to their overall energy level being higher than usual or lower than usual, depending on the need or the circumstances. Not only is it a socially accepted conversation at work, in social circles and in the doctor's office, it's also a good measure for understanding how we feel in the aggregate in lieu of examining how we feel at each level.

To go a step deeper, many will admit in casual conversation that they have a difficult time relaxing without a glass of wine or sleeping without the assistance of some smoke or a pill. Some will acknowledge the gnawing level of anxiety that rarely, if ever, fully abates. Then there are those who will know that his or her leg bounces up and down at a rapid pace while seated but feel stumped when asked why. Collectively, we have come to accept these situations as the way things are, and we've even found our dysfunctions to be useful in commiserating with others. That certainly is a silver lining, but it's not a cause for languishing in the acceptance that our discomforts are just the way things are. It is difficult to know if a symptom is the result of daily wear and tear or a result of an unrealized trauma, injury or undiagnosed illness. But, even in cases where you have symptoms as the result of those more imbedded reasons, wear and tear is still having an impact on the way you feel. Of course, in some cases symptoms will be the result of traumas, injuries, or illness, and there are many books on those subjects. But before straining oneself on assuming the worst, an equally good place to start is to look at the quality of energy self-care given in a daily practice of Reiki. Even if it doesn't provide all the answers, it does provide relief.

To be sure, rare is the case that someone is doing their best when it comes to their personal self-care regime. This doesn't make us bad; it makes us human. It doesn't even make us bad humans, still — just human. The truth is, it's hard to take care of yourself. There are no prizes given for best self-care. No one has ever been called a good person because they take such good care of themselves. That accolade is given mostly to those who sacrifice their own needs to provide for others — even when we know that's an unsustainable practice. Our value system got it backwards and, in the process, ends up diminishing self-sustainment to reward self-sacrifice.

Now, that is not to say that we shouldn't help others, of course we should, if we can. But help is always best delivered when individual performance is optimized. When seen this way, self-care becomes a worthy and virtuous goal. To provide the best quality self-care not only to feel better but to help others to do the same is not only individually sustainable, it creates a healthier community.

Reiki, if you use it, can help you achieve your self-care goals. Its value as a self-care practice falls gently into the "as above, so below" concept that, applied in this context, suggests that the general health and well-being of the subtler aspects of experience corresponds to the more solid aspects of experience. By providing energy remedy and repair to the physical body and the aura, imbalances due to daily wear and tear are avoided, minimized, if not impeded from graduating into larger, more disruptive imbalances. By providing remedy and repair to daily wear and tear, tensions are abated. It is not only easier to relax, the volatility of one's emotions is minimized, leaving a sense of balance that engenders greater mental clarity. These benefits in subtler areas ripple outward and we feel better.

While students come to Reiki for various reasons, it's worth accepting that at its core, a pursuit of Reiki practice shows a desire to feel better, whatever that means for you, for it will mean different things to different people. Still, most will agree on the basics, which include a desire to sleep better, feel more balanced, and have more energy at the end of a long day. So, if everyone agrees that it's better to feel better, and that the more we give ourselves the more we have to give to others, then a quality, comprehensive daily self-care regime becomes an easier personal commitment to make. While that may seem daunting, I humbly suggest that if you have a Reiki attunement, at some point whether acutely aware of it or not, you already chose to make that commitment. You chose to try again, to do what you can to feel better for you. The hardest part, which was choosing you, is done. What's left now and what it's time to get into, is practice, every day. When you consider that better self-care can be had by anyone and is a worthy goal for everyone, all you are left to ask yourself is, *What am I waiting for?* And with that, we move to Part II – In Practice.

PART II

In Practice

Introduction

Welcome to your Reiki practice, and don't worry if it's been a while. Whether you've been attuned recently or some time ago, starting a consistent daily practice is a bit of an uphill challenge. That's just a fact for most people; present company included. That's right, when I first started, I was so excited after my attunement that I used it every day throughout my adjustment period. But as the days and weeks went on, I started to miss a day here and there, and before I knew it, my daily practice fell off altogether.

If you are one of the few who enjoy a consistent, daily practice, then you're already experiencing the value that practice brings to your well-being. But if you aren't, that doesn't mean you don't value Reiki or want it in your life; it just means you have yet to develop the habits that help bring practice into your daily routine. But don't worry, this Part II is here to help, and help it will. So, regardless of when your journey into Reiki started or if and how often you practice, let's start where the attunement class likely left off: the beginning of daily practice.

As we discussed in the essays in Part I, the key to committing to our Reiki practice is rooted in us establishing value for it. Now, that we've done that, the next key, the one to ensuring practice beyond our best intentions, desires and strongest commitments, is found by building confidence in and through practice. To be sure, confidence and well-being are the result of daily practice, but before that, practice is a leap of faith filled with hope. This makes the goal of Part II to help students move from hope to lasting self-assurance by explaining how to practice, highlighting perceived internal impediments to practice, dispelling external factors that can impede practice, and setting expectations to start again when you stop.

These essays are written to go deeper than how to practice. They are written to help students understand what barriers make them stop and how to transcend those so that daily practice becomes their new natural default. Like rolling waves that gently but effectively wear down stone, these articles are written to gently but effectively wear down the reasons and protestations that can keep daily practice just out of reach. But as a start, it's good to remember that you can love Reiki and still fail to keep up with regular practice, so this is no place to feel bad about that. It's remarkably common to meet a well-intentioned student who leans on the hope that someday they'll pick their practice back up, when confidence would be the better stabilizing force, not to mention, the better beacon for practice. So, let's do that. Let's review how to practice, and then through practice build up our confidence, which will then in turn make daily practice an easy-to-do, feel-better exercise. But tuck in and get comfortable here, because lasting confidence can't be gained in a single session or in sporadic practice. Building confidence takes time, but most importantly it takes repetition. In short, it takes practice. While Reiki as a practice is not a time-consuming exercise, building confidence in it is. Practice is an essential building block to gaining confidence, and confidence gained will encourage more practice. It's a tidy little circle, and before you know it, your practice will become second nature; a daily habit you rarely think about but know in your heart you couldn't do without.

So, with that, let's practice.

> "The power to heal oneself is extraordinary and mundane. It's also a responsibility and a gift.

The Reiki Cupped Hand Position

Reiki flows from a cupped hand. Like engaging a faucet, the cupped hand position is what starts the flow of Reiki. If there is anything that, in a sense, "turns Reiki on," it's the cupped hand position. Once engaged or formed, whichever terminology you prefer, Reiki will flow. So, to be clear, there is a hand position that starts the flow of Reiki. Cupped Reiki hand: Reiki on; flat hand: Reiki off — this of course, is only made possible after a Reiki attunement.

Generally, this hand position is something your teacher will teach you following your attunement. First you become a channel, and then you learn how to engage this new ability you now have. Still, if this is the first time you've heard of the cupped hand position, don't worry. If you are a student who has been practicing for some time with a flat-ish hand, don't worry. And lastly, if you are a teacher who hasn't taught the cupped hand position or has done so inconsistently, don't worry. This is an easy thing to remedy. To be fair, the teachings of the Reiki cupped hand position have been inconsistent in some cases and lost altogether in others, and this is not the fault of any one Reiki teacher. However, it is worth examining why it has been lost, or in some cases, forgotten altogether, for with that information we can find our way back. While there are many reasons that can provide insight and offer explanation, I'll stick to the two that I propose have had the most substantive impact. The first is that Reiki is taught as an oral tradition, and the second is that the teaching of its practice is demonstrative.

Firstly, as an oral tradition, the study of Reiki has in many ways become a growing game of Telephone. The game of Telephone is generally played by a group of people. It starts with everyone sitting in a circle, and then one designated person whispers a message into the ear of the person who is sitting to their immediate right. That person then whispers the message into the next person's ear and so forth. The game ends when the last person to receive the whispered message declares the message they heard. The group then generally erupts in laughter, as by the time the original message has reached the last person it has changed, and in most cases has changed dramatically and hysterically. This has been both an intended and unintended consequence in Reiki. Intended, in that as the teaching of Reiki spread out from rural Japan into a larger world with many differing cultures, changes were made that best met the teaching values and cultural norms throughout the world. Unintended, in that some key tenets of its teaching have been lost, so to speak, in translation. Additionally, even in a lineage where the cupped hand position is regularly taught, it can only take one teacher who misses it on just one occasion to inadvertently change the course of instruction as it is passed down.

Secondly, as a demonstrative practice, precision counts, and like in the example above, all it takes is for one well-intended and dedicated Reiki teacher to feel tired at the end of the day and erringly demonstrate Reiki with an overly relaxed hand. Just one instance of this can change the way countless numbers of students will be taught in the years to follow. It takes so little to rewrite how something is taught, especially in an oral tradition, and as teachings are received from a qualified and dedicated teacher, the new way rightly becomes a known and respected aspect of practice. So much so, that it can be hard to change or try something that could challenge what is considered conventional wisdom. This makes any resistance to trying the cupped hand position easy to understand and yet, the only way to truly know the difference the Reiki cupped hand position can make to your Reiki practice is to try it. As with all things mentioned in this book, I encourage the reader to test it out for yourself, and not just once. Commit to a week and see how you feel. It will cost you nothing to try, and it can be the difference between you feeling that Reiki is working and you feeling that Reiki isn't.

In all transparency, I've seen students who all but abandoned practice, physically jump in surprise and awe after some gentle encouragement to try the cupped hand position helped them feel a steady, heavier flow of Reiki come through. Most students will be drawn to try the cupped hand position through curiosity while others may willfully reject the suggestion. And to be fair, change of any kind can be hard, and if for you Reiki is already a beloved practice, I not only understand the hesitation, I proceed with great care in my encouragement of the cupped hand because I think it's better to practice with a flat hand than to not practice at all. To be clear, if you've been attuned to Reiki and utilize a flat or flat-ish hand to practice, I'm not suggesting that Reiki isn't flowing out to some degree; it is. However, the flow of Reiki is made all the more successful and consistent by the cupped hand position.

As previously mentioned, the cupped hand position can be likened to turning on a faucet that Reiki flows through. The hand position is the mechanism that starts the flow of Reiki. While you may receive some Reiki from a flatter, less turned-on position, it's considerably less than would otherwise flow by being fully turned on. A bit like a faucet of water that drips or lightly streams out instead of a strong and consistent flow. The cupped hand position is a faucet that turns on the flow of Reiki, and using it properly will help to amplify both the feeling of Reiki and the benefits of practice.

To get started and to feel confident that your cupped hand is correct, consider that the cupped hand position resembles its namesake, a cup. For students who learn visually, you can imagine using your hand to hold water and that, for the most part, is the shape you're looking for. For those who learn by doing, I've found a more direct, tactile way to the cupped hand position, which makes using it easier. The cupped hand position for Reiki follows many of the natural curves of the physical body. This means students can use certain parts of their body as the mold to gently shape the hand into the optimal cupped hand position.

To do this start by gently keeping your fingers together, including the thumb – keep the hand soft and moldable, and then gently mold the hand around the curve of your opposing shoulder. The hand needs to be soft and moldable with enough tension to hold the position properly. If seated, the student can also use the round of the knee to gently mold the hand into position, but it doesn't stop there. The curve of the neck works, as does the crown of the head. Any time you've held the round of your forehead as a means to comfort you from exhaustion or headache, your hand has been molded into the Reiki cupped hand position. The curves of your body inform the cupped hand position, and it's all you need to form it or re-form it if the hand has become relaxed and mildly flattened over the course of practice.

If you have an injury or your fingers are shaped in a way that makes it difficult or impossible to keep the fingers, including the thumb, together, then do what's comfortable for your hand first, and beyond that, don't worry. Giving Reiki should not be a painful exercise, and a relaxed moldable hand is of greater value to the cupped hand position than a strict, unsustainable adherence to the form itself. Reiki will work within the structure of your hand, and so any injury or immobility to a finger or a joint will not inhibit practice. I feel that worth repeating. The cupped hand position is not about seeking perfection in shape. If you have limited movement for one reason or another or your hand has trouble making the perfect cupped shape, don't worry — Reiki will still flow. Just do your best, relax and gently practice. It will work for you. I've had many students with similar issues try and succeed with no problems. Erika lost the upper part of a finger. Gianna suffers from mild arthritis and has difficulty bringing her thumb in against her forefinger. Ryan has a damaged finger joint that doesn't allow his finger to bend, and Dev has a finger that's been fused and so can't unbend. Each of these students have a successful Reiki practice. Here, I'll also briefly mention that you only need one hand to practice, not two — but I'll get into that in a later essay.

If you aren't already, consider using the cupped hand position now as you read along. To begin, place your left hand — keeping the fingers and thumb as together as you can — around the natural curve of your right shoulder. Or go right to left, whichever is most comfortable. As you do, your hand will mold around the natural curve of the shoulder and into the Reiki cupped hand position. Now gently lift your hand from the shoulder, keeping it in the cupped position. The shoulder helped to mold and hold it in front of you with the palm side of your cupped hand facing up. It will look as if its capable of holding water — and it is! This is the Reiki cupped hand position. Now, to begin self-treatment, simply turn your hand towards your body and allow it to rest on the body or hover above. By doing this, you are practicing Reiki.

If for any reason, you find it's not comfortable using the shoulder, you can also use the top of your head as a mold or the round of your neck. If you're sitting, you can use the ball of your knee. The natural curves of the body are the most natural way to establish and re-establish the cupped hand position for Reiki. I say re-establish because as mentioned before, it's common during self-treatment for your cupped hand to become relaxed along with the rest of you and slowly begin to flatten as you practice. Equally, it's natural to expect that endurance sustaining the position will be a challenge, especially when giving Reiki to another. If you notice during practice that your cupped hand is starting to look a bit tent-ish or is going flat, don't worry. Gently use the shoulder, knee, round of the neck or top of the head as a mold to help you restore the integrity of the position. With practice, it's fair to expect that your level of endurance with the position will increase to the point where it will feel so natural that it becomes a new self-sustaining and replenishing habit.

To better understand the cupped hand position in terms of form, it can be helpful to think of its strong and moldable structure as a marriage of relaxation and tension. Meaning that while some tension is applied to maintain the form, it is a natural tension, made possible through a state of relative relaxation and so creates balance and symmetry in the form. Stress or an excess of tension applied to the position is relatively common and generally the result of a good student wanting to ensure success by unintentionally overdoing it in an attempt to do well. Generally, these are earnest, well-intentioned students who go into practice with more vigor than is necessary but for the right reasons. This overdoing of the position is generally evidenced when the natural curve of the cupped hand position becomes more rigid and tent-shaped, like that of an upside-down right angle. The tent-like shape is considerably less conducive for practicing Reiki, but if you notice your hands have become more rigid or angled, don't worry, you've got everything you need to restore your cupped hand position. Simply take a moment to breathe, and once again use the natural curves of your body to establish an active, yet relaxed cupped hand and continue on with treatment.

The more it's practiced, the more natural the practice of it becomes. It will also help bring Reiki into daily practice by making Reiki itself more accessible. I often see my students sitting with cupped hands gently laid in their lap, some not having noticed it until I've mentioned it. Other students have emailed me to share their own discovery of finding Reiki hands gently placed in the lap while watching television or in a meeting. To me, that's the best kind of practice, the kind that feels as natural as getting a glass of water from instinct, before you've mentally acknowledged thirst.

I do have one caveat that I haven't mentioned yet because it's not about the cupped Reiki hand, but it is about practice: something that impedes flow when it's done while practicing is crossing any body part. By that, I mean crossing your legs or your arms, both common stances while sitting or standing. In energetic and physical terms, crossing is a protective stance. It's done to fortify or stabilize a position, even if it's done unconsciously as part of an old habit. I mention it here to say that if you are sitting in a crossed-leg position or have anything crossed while practicing, you may notice that Reiki isn't flowing as it usually does. Thankfully, this is also a simple fix: simply uncross what is crossed and Reiki will flow once again unimpeded.

Now armed with more information than you ever thought existed about the cupped hand position, many questions have been answered, leaving one question, directed at you. If you're not already practicing the cupped hand position, will you try? To be certain, there is nothing to lose and much to gain, but it is best tried on your own terms and in your own time.

In the meantime, I wish for you the wonder and excitement I've seen in the eyes of so many who have tried. But more than that, I wish for you a strong and consistent Reiki practice on whatever terms you decide are best.

> *To be sure, you think you got this, but you don't. Don't worry, it's an easy fix.*

Coming-to-Terms Moments: Working Through Internal Inhibitors of Practice

If you had your attunement in the physical presence of a teacher, you have been permanently attuned. This means that the positive changes made to your energy system through the action of attunement — changes that enabled you to be a channel for Reiki — remain unchanged. Once attuned, you're attuned, you're always attuned, neither time nor lack of activity can change that. If years have passed since you've practiced, there is no need to worry, your next Reiki experience is only a cupped hand away. You may feel a bit out of practice; that's to be expected, but Reiki will flow.

So, now that our worry about our attunement is behind us, how do we get from no practice to daily practice? We start by understanding the invisible external factors and internal pressures that stand between us and practice.

To be sure, there will be external factors that, at times, make committing to practice feel more challenging. By external factors, I mean things that appear to sit just outside your span of control, like demands on your time or the needs that other have of you. However, understanding the requirements of a Reiki practice, or lack thereof, often helps to melt away the restriction these external factors present, making both practice possible and Reiki accessible.

This is good news indeed, but with that said, I've found time and time again that before a discussion on external factors can be valuable for students, it's both necessary and helpful for teachers to acknowledge and discuss the internal pressures that are more often than not the true impediment to daily practice first. I call these internal pressures *coming-to-terms moments,* and it's in the transcendence of those moments that the road to consistent daily practice is paved. While for some, these coming-to-terms moments may seem like natural transitions that are easily traversed, others, at first glance, may consider these coming-to-terms moments unnecessary, as they seem too obvious for contemplation. To be fair, most students are sure to dismiss this, but I encourage all students to lean in, because it is these seemingly obvious moments that stand between well-intentioned students and regular practice. More so in fact than any external pressure or demand, it is just that the external pressure and demands feel all the more real and so become the obvious points to blame. To be brutally concise, if you think you got this, chances are you don't have this, and even if you do, understanding these coming-to-terms moments will help you understand what stands in the way of many others. Additionally, the more you know about how to use Reiki, the more the pressure of external factors will naturally fade. So again, lean in, because the coming-to-terms moments are the more pressing concern, but rest assured, each one can be easily met and transcended.

Coming-to-terms moments serve as the bridge that empowers students to go from knowing what is good for them to doing what it is good for them. Now, before that gets to sounding too heavy or too responsibility-focused, it can also be seen as fun, like an adventure or an exploration of your own self-awareness, or a journey that takes you from learning to knowing to being. It's for this reason I often start my classes by explaining that if Reiki is a destination, it's one paved with coming-to-terms moments. And it's a journey that begins the moment someone places Reiki in your hands and comes to completion when Reiki practice becomes a natural and unfettered part of your daily life. As you have already started your journey, allow me to narrate and explain this part of the coming-to-terms path.

To be clear, coming-to-terms moments are not a Reiki exclusive. Coming-to-terms moments are inherent to all learning. They are a necessary, productive and integral part of the learning process and of establishing adherence of a new practice. A coming-to-terms moment is an inner doing of the student, whereby he or she acknowledges and accepts what has been learned, while allowing inner resistances, such as self-doubt, fear of change, and even fear of success, to gently wane. It is this doing that makes integration of what has been learned possible. In other words, the backside of coming-to-terms moments is where doubt has been transcended, leaving acceptance and a spark of confidence. Without these moments, students may understand the theory, but daily practice will feel out of reach, making coming-to-terms moments the small but significant hurdle that sits between theory and practice.

In short, a coming-to-terms moment is allowing what is, to be. In Reiki, an example of a coming-to-terms moment is in the calmness that follows the sparks of feelings that result from any of the statements listed below:

- When I use Reiki, I feel calm.
- I feel Reiki coming out of my hand.
- I feel heat coming out of your hand as you give me Reiki.
- I used Reiki all week and I feel energized.
- When I use Reiki before bed, I sleep better.

While the idea of allowing what is to be may sound simple enough, it is important to acknowledge that it's not simple at all. In truth, people are prone to the opposite. Instead of coming to terms with what is and allowing what is to be, people are prone to overexplain, dissect and attempt to control what is. When that's not sufficient, people have the tendency to escalate to argument (this includes arguments within the self) and attempt to either alter what is or bend the will of another until it is agreed that what is, is what we think it ought to be, instead of what is. This is often done as a means of conformity. People tend to value fitting in above much else. In fact, the seeds of self-doubt are often born from a desire to fit in with others. You cannot underestimate how sought-out the self-doubter's club is or how hard it recruits. As a result, we have the tendency to leap when we need to relax, to do when we need to be, and to suffer when we can be well. This can be remedied by allowing what is to be without feeling driven to define, manipulate or control it, mentally speaking or otherwise.

To be sure, the mind will accept what is with greater ease than it will attempt to control it. Exerting control adds to our already full workload, but because our habits bring us into control mode, we tend to think control is our default. It's not. It can be a hard habit to give up, but it's a worthy one to try and you can do so. Rest assured that there will still be plenty on your list that you will need to control, without Reiki being one of them. To that end, when it comes to Reiki, it can be helpful to view a coming-to-terms moment as an adjustment of sorts, a reconciliation and acceptance of what has changed or what is felt energetically. To help, what follows are three coming-to-terms moments worth mentioning, as these are three that every student can expect to see.

> **The first coming-to-terms moment worth mentioning is the one that comes in accepting that following a Reiki attunement, you are channel for Reiki.**

What this means is that when you place your hand in the cupped position, Reiki flows out. To be clear, receiving an attunement does not give you the power to make Reiki; instead, it creates the energetic change needed to allow you to become a channel for it, in a similar way that a hose is a channel for water to flow through. Before the Reiki attunement, you were not a channel for Reiki, and now following the Reiki attunement, you are. While this was a chosen experience and one that the student has put effort into having, it's still a remarkable change and one that can take a minute (or more) to get used to, so I encourage students to take a moment and come to terms with this remarkable change. It may on the surface seems like a small one, but it's a significant change that places the power of healing, quite literally, in the palm of your hands.

On several occasions, I've even had students remark, half in jest, at how having the ability to channel Reiki feels like having a superpower. I think that statement is neither something to be laughed off or dismissed. It is a remarkable new ability, and while it certainly doesn't match the super-human powers seen in the stories of our comic book heroes, it is indeed, super. Allowing time for this moment to set in, be it a minute, a day, a week or a series of moments over time, is an important step in helping the student realize the empowerment and added self-sufficiency that follows an attunement.

> **The next coming-to-terms moment worth mentioning is in the realization that Reiki works.**

Just like the last one, this coming-to-terms moment is just as straightforward but equally as compelling and often overlooked. Reiki works, and if it's used, Reiki will help you feel better. If you think about it, that's a superpower, and it's the sort of stuff often found in fantasy fiction. But let's put that to the side for just a moment, because while the obviousness of this coming-to-terms moment may at first appear to render it obsolete, especially when you consider that students come to a Reiki attunement because they believe it works, it's not. Consider that it's often the case that what we hope will be true, still more often than not surprises us when we actually experience it to be true. Such a surprise can blossom into excitement, but it can also lead to fear, and fear, especially when left unrecognized, often leads to paralysis, which in the case of Reiki causes the student to stop using the very thing they spent time learning. It is for this reason that while it may appear that I'm preaching to the already converted, even the converted who are among the most enthusiastic can find themselves surprised, and in some cases unnerved or even scared when using Reiki in those first days and beyond.

I've got a good example that helps me illustrate this. I'm sure most teachers will have similar tales to tell. Kimberly, one of my advanced students, is known for saying and sometimes exclaiming, "Reiki is weird! It's just weird! I mean, it's amazing but it's weird." She says this with jubilance and reverence but with a funny, nervous sort of smile on her face, that seems to say, "I don't know if I'll ever really understand this." She also appears visibly perplexed by it. Of course, she says this as a means to put herself and other students at ease, and it's always followed by laughter and nods of agreement around the room, and I'm always glad for this. This student, who at the time of this writing has just started her master's trainings, is warm, funny and kind. Self-admittedly a cynic at the start, Kimberly came to the practice with lots of hope and a dash of desperation but also was a bit unsure, cautious even, like someone who was afraid to put time into something that resulted in another disappointing outcome.

What she found, happily, was that Reiki works, and now it's become an indispensable part of her daily self-care. Next, she had to come to terms with having a new power with which to help herself. Now a master and after years of practice, she can still find herself feeling gleefully freaked out by it. She's made it a practice to lean into these moments with humor, enjoying Reiki more and settling into the responsibility of using it. Her example demonstrates a strong personal commitment to doing what she can to feel better, and her gentle, if not humorous persistence of practice is what lay at the core of this unique coming-to-terms moment.

> **The third coming-to-terms moment worth mentioning is that Reiki works on demand.**

Which is to say that once attuned, you are free to use Reiki when you choose to or when you have demand for it. To arrive at this coming-to-terms moment, you must successfully come to terms with the first two moments mentioned previously. You have come to terms with the fact that you are a channel of Reiki and know for yourself, through personal experience, that Reiki works. What comes next is a coming-to-terms moment anchored in personal responsibility. It's the recognition and acceptance that it's up to you to know when and how often you use Reiki, for Reiki can only work for you, if you use it. Again, the obviousness of this statement is clear, but I often say to students and clients alike, "Just because something's clear, doesn't mean it's easy." To be sure, knowing that it's your responsibility to practice Reiki doesn't make establishing practice easy.

While this coming-to-terms moment acknowledges that you alone control when you practice, that acknowledgment is also accompanied by a cacophony of reasonable reasons, or excuses, for why you haven't got around to it. Like the previous coming-to-terms moment, there are some fears to face here. Those worth mentioning include: the fear that you'll forget to practice, the fear of not doing it right, and the fear that making time for practice comes at the expense of something else or, even worse, someone else. This is usually when our fears call upon its faithful companion, guilt, which both distracts and redirects us. Suddenly, the student may find themselves feeling a bit guilty for making time to practice, guilty for doing something for themselves when others need them, and even feeling a bit guilty for feeling better than others.

What I speak of here are the feelings of fear and guilt based more on our perceptions and less on reality itself, and this is a key point. Our perceptions are mostly a personal experience. While some perceptions can be shared, for the most part, our perception is our own and for good reason. It is our perception that provides us with the well-meaning narrative we use to help us define our individual experience. Generally, perception is a combination of our culturally shared reality plus the individual's insecurities and overcompensations. The result being that while some students may share the same guilty feeling about practice, others may feel guilty but about different aspects of practice, including feeling better. This makes this coming-to-terms moment a bit different from the other two because it's more of a perceptual one that calls our bluff by begging the question, now that we have gone through the trouble and expense to become attuned, what are we going to do with it?

Of course, the answer to that question is practice, but such an answer is hardly enough to help most students begin and sustain a daily practice. I regularly notice experienced students come to class in the hope that Reiki will work for them more than they come confident in their experience of practice. These are often students who are committed to the idea of Reiki, but their reliance on hope reveals a lack of coming to terms, even as interest in study persists. This can be because the obviousness of these coming-to-terms moments often leave them unexplored. The coming-to-terms moments seem too simple to apply to the students' experiences, and, therefore, become taken for granted. However, the problem inherent in languishing on the hope of Reiki over coming to terms with it is that it often results in a lack of practice. The student who leans on hope is often unaware that it masks a temporary conflict or, better said, a momentary confoundment with allowing what is, when it comes to Reiki and practice, to be. When this is the case, I gently and once again encourage the student to lean in and offer the gentle reminder that for most, taking good care of yourself is a confronting commitment to make. It's the reason that once value is well-established for Reiki, my focus turns to the value of building confidence through practice, and that begins with confronting and reconciling these coming-to-terms moments.

It may happen in moments or take some time, but once you've ascended this trifecta of coming-to-terms moments, you're likely to see your excitement for Reiki mature into a sobriety for it. Practice brings forward the power of sobriety, the deep inner knowing that feels more grounded and mundane than unique or important. Similar to the sobriety you have for daily dental hygiene, its root is in acceptance; not only for the need of care but in the benefits of it. This sobriety will help keep you buoyant and tuned to practice, which will help because once you're set with your motivation and commitment to practice, you'll have the rest of your world to contend with. That is when the external forces that define the hectic nature of your life, as well as the demands others have on your time, will initially appear to compete with the work required to establish this new, self-sustaining habit. But even here, there's good news.

While at times, beginning practice will start to feel like something you'd like to do but don't have the time for, you do. When it comes to Reiki, you can, in a sense, really have it all. You can have a Reiki practice and a full-time, non-yielding life. In fact, one helps the fulfillment of the other. Which is to say that once you've come to terms with Reiki, you can relax and take the pressure of practice off by learning how to incorporate Reiki as something that makes the hectic nature of your life more manageable, instead of something you have to add to an already busy schedule.

> *Rethink what's necessary for practice, so that you can come to it with greater ease.*

Working Through the External Factors That Appear to Impede Practice

With so many demands on daily life, starting a new self-care practice seems like a luxury to some, an impossibility to others, and something the rest of us swear we'll get around to as soon as we can. Reiki, however, does not need to be one of those self-care practices we'll get to one day because unlike other self-care practices, Reiki has few external factors that act as a barrier to practice. This is often a surprising revelation to students, but it's true. For example, the predominant barrier believed to impede practice is that a student needs to make time for practice, but that's not true with Reiki. Reiki can be practiced throughout the day and alongside other activities. This makes Reiki readily accessible and takes the pressure off of having to find time to practice.

To that end, it is helpful to keep in mind that healing is a daily activity that comes in many forms, and most daily healing occurs as a result of everyday self-care practices. Practices like drinking water, eating foods that aid in digestion, getting enough activity each day, exercising good personal hygiene and getting enough rest. In fact, advanced healing and medical interventions often — not always, but often enough to be worth mentioning — become necessary when the quality of self-care practices wane, unintentionally become abandoned, ignored, or done in smaller doses than is needed. Stressful lifestyle choices that make meeting our basic self-care needs harder can further exacerbate budding imbalances, tipping them into illness or injury. This suggests what we all know to be true, which is when stressors become larger, louder and a bigger part of a daily life, more self-care is needed, not less.

But still, too few of us can keep up with our daily self-care needs, and when we struggle, Reiki is generally the first self-care practice we abandon. It becomes a slippery slope after that, and before we know it, we've traded our water for coffee, our vegetables for salty snacks and the next thing we know is that we're sleeping less and feeling more irritable. As simple as it sounds, Reiki can help turn that terrible tide and return us to a state of better self-care and balance.

But first, let us acknowledge that for those who struggle in their commitment to daily practice, time is often the top factor cited to explain why. And, to be fair, who doesn't struggle with having enough time for yourself? If you're living, you're likely struggling with this now or have. This struggle can make starting practice difficult because despite best intentions, making time for it is hard. For example, a yoga practice, meditation, a martial arts class, working out, even preparing a nourishing meal requires time set aside, but Reiki is different. Unlike those self-care practices, Reiki can be practiced alongside other activities, and it can be done inconspicuously, making it something that can be practiced both publicly and privately. This means that not only can Reiki be practiced at a set time each day if that's your preference, but it can be practiced in scattered segments throughout your day, making it both accessible and easy to use.

With that in mind, what follows are three valuable insights that further explain why this is true and how to use this information to incorporate practice into that over-the-top-with-things-to-do life of yours. If this information is new to you, don't worry, it's all good news and information you can use immediately and test for yourself. What follows is meant to help you make a fresh start with practice, not to question past reasons for what got in the way. So please, proceed gently.

Reiki doesn't require a meditative state

Our first insight is the game changer, because it directly addresses both a common misconception about Reiki as well as the time element that often impedes practice. Reiki doesn't require a meditative state. That's worth saying again, Reiki doesn't require a meditative state. In other words, the student does not need to be in a meditative state for Reiki to work. This is because Reiki does not use nor is directly influenced by your state of mind. At the same time, meditating while practicing Reiki will not influence Reiki, because again, Reiki is not influenced by your state of mind. This comes as a surprise to many who think they either have to mentally focus on practice or go into a meditative state for Reiki to work. This information may also distress those who teach Reiki as a form of meditation, however, Reiki is not meditation. The benefits of Reiki will certainly aid a person in achieving a meditative state, making a meditative state easier to attain and all the more fulfilling, but that does not make Reiki meditation. Reiki is Reiki and meditation is meditation, and while both yield significant self-care benefits, neither practice requires intersection with the other for it to work. This is immediately testable, and while it may feel strange or different at first, I encourage you test it and then test it again and again. To test this, simply give yourself Reiki without going into a meditative state. If you have been practicing while reading along, you've been doing this.

Moreover, the fact that Reiki works without requiring a meditative state is a key point to understand because some natural healing vibrations do require a meditative state, and for vibrations to be effective, time does need to be set aside for practice. However, because Reiki is not one of those, it does not. Now, what sets Reiki apart from natural healing vibrations that require a meditative state is that Reiki does not utilize brain wave activity, nor does it intersect by way of providing healing to the mind or, as some healers may call it, the mental body.

To put this in physical context, imagine if a meditative state was required for the act of flossing your teeth. This would impose a considerable time restraint while offering no real benefit. While both practices are certainly valuable exercises in self-care, they don't naturally intersect, and their forced intersection makes neither practice better nor more useful. This fact should take nothing away from either of these practices because it positively delivers value to both.

Reiki can be an inconspicuous practice

The next insight is that Reiki can be an inconspicuous practice. This means you could potentially practice Reiki anywhere and no one around you would even notice. It does that by revealing that Reiki flows naturally and with ease from a cupped Reiki hand, but that doesn't mean you need to use both hands to practice. One hand will do. You're welcome to use both hands, but it's not required for Reiki to work or for practice to be successful or complete. This is helpful to understand because it further supports Reiki being practiced alongside other activities.

It can also provide peace of mind to students who want to practice but may have an injured hand or simply have some discomfort that makes using one hand doable, but not both. I share this insight with great care because students are taught and encouraged to use both hands in practice. This is done as a best practice measure: if you have two, why not use both? However, there may be occasions when the use of both hands is not possible or inconvenient. Teaching Reiki as a two-handed practice is logical when two hands are available, but teaching it as a two-handed practice was never intended to infer that two hands were necessary for practice. One hand placed in the cupped Reiki position will do.

Sequencing

The final insight may also appear to break with convention, but upon closer scrutiny it does not — it simply provides clarity. In fact, once understood it makes a lot of sense and is likely something that as a student you have already found to be true. Reiki does not have to be given in any set place or position on the body for practice to occur. Your cupped Reiki hand placed anywhere on the body is enough. Accordingly, practice does not need to follow a particular sequence of placements along the body.

Hand placements and sequencing (also known as hand positions) are often taught as a means to provide structure to a new student, in the hope that the structure will help the student build confidence by having a blueprint to follow. It's a blueprint that has value, but only if it does not inadvertently create a barrier to daily practice. Sadly, however, in our busy world, it has, and that's the reason why I address it. Hand placements and sequencing is a tool for teaching, not a requirement for practice. Understanding this also helps by providing peace of mind to students who may not be able to reach or feel comfortable giving Reiki to the lower extremities of the body. To be clear, placing your cupped Reiki hand anywhere on or in the direction of your body is enough. That alone is practice, and that is all that is needed to receive Reiki and all its benefits.

You're welcome to follow the blueprint that sequencing provides because you may enjoy doing so, and if that is the case, please continue. Just rest assured, that while following the prescribed sequencing may be enjoyable, it's not necessary for practice. While the hope of sequencing is to help students build confidence by providing a guide to follow, its shortfall is threefold and worthy of a full explanation.

Sequencing's Three Shortfalls

Sequencing's first shortfall is that it requires a time commitment that most students simply don't have. When a student feels he or she can't meet the time commitment necessary for practice, the commitment to practice, regardless of how helpful the practice is believed to be, wanes.

Its second shortfall is that students are taught, almost in the same breath, that Reiki goes where it's needed most. This is correct: Reiki does go where it's needed most, which is an extraordinary benefit of the practice. However, it also inadvertently contradicts sequencing and leaves students asking, "Then why I am giving myself Reiki in a set of places if it goes where it's needed most?" Over the years, this question has left a few teachers stumped themselves. The answer is that the purpose of sequencing is as a teaching tool and a confidence builder, not a delivery system of Reiki making stops at major hubs where Reiki is needed. To be clear, sequencing is not the tool that delivers Reiki — your cupped hand does that. It's also not the tool that receives Reiki — that's the body.

The third and last shortfall of sequencing is that some students will have difficulty meeting all its instructions, most particularly the bending required to deliver Reiki to the lower extremities.

With that said, if you enjoy the sequencing method, by all means use it to feel, learn and experience. It's a system that provides each student with the opportunity to feel Reiki, and perhaps explore their own sensitivities, as the student may start to notice that it's easier to feel Reiki in some areas when compared to others. Because sequencing begins at the top of the body (the head) and moves down, eventually ending at the bottom (the feet), students may find areas of the body that are more sensitive to sensation than others. For example, the sensation of Reiki may be easier to feel behind the eyes than on the ball of the knee cap. It can make the exploration of Reiki all the more enjoyable — that is of course, when time permits. Sequencing also gives the student a sense of what is considered a complete Reiki session. For students interested in moving into a Reiki level-2 practice, this can make sequencing an invaluable tool in its effort to help new students build confidence, both in a personal practice as well as a practice serving others. For these reasons, I encourage all students to follow sequencing when time permits, and I'd like to underline that sentiment. *When time permits*, because it is best that sequencing is seen for what it is, a luxury of practice, not a requirement of it. To be sure, sequencing can aid in learning but should not become an impediment to daily practice when time is limited. When time is limited, and it often is, a cupped hand gently placed on your lap or applied to your head or anywhere really, is sufficient for practice and yes, you are doing it right. You are practicing Reiki.

But whether you're pro-sequencing or not, what is certain is that your cupped Reiki hand placed anywhere on or in the direction of your body was all that was ever needed. That, in a nutshell, is practice. This paired with the other insights frees up students to practice Reiki anytime and anywhere it feels suitable and comfortable to do so. Recommendations for how to do just that include practicing Reiki by placing your cupped Reiki hand on your lap during a meeting or in class, or gently resting your cupped Reiki hand on your hip while standing in the elevator, or standing in line. You can practice while reading or while enjoying a movie by gently laying your cupped Reiki hand on your lap or side. Practice while having tea with a friend or while sitting in the dentist's chair — that can certainly be a time when Reiki can make an uncomfortable experience easier to bear. Practice can be had at the next PTA meeting, or while cheering the kids on at their next sporting event or recital. Placing your cupped Reiki hand in the manners suggested above is inconspicuous and appears rather natural, so no one is even likely to notice.

Practice is what lies at the heart of every Reiki course. Regardless of what is taught and what is learned, Reiki can only support you when it's practiced. There will be no point in your Reiki study when practice will become obsolete or unnecessary. Practice is the goal, the mantra, the very point of its teaching, and Reiki, by its nature, makes practice easily accessible. This is good news to remember on days when it feels like there is little time and lots to do. It's not necessary to set aside time solely for the purpose of Reiki practice. Reiki isn't fussed and takes no offense if it has to share your attention and focus. Reiki practice is meant to support you in the relentlessness of your life, and it requires little from you to make it work. But if you do make it work, before you know it, it will become a habit, and soon you may start to find yourself sitting with a cupped Reiki hand on your lap without noticing yourself doing it. I've seen this in my students many times, and this is a great gift indeed. It's your body's way of saying that it appreciates the self-care.

Furthermore, unlike the slippery slope mentioned earlier, daily practice creates an ascendant cascade that has a positive ripple effect on the quality of all self-care practices. This boost of sorts is one we all need, especially during the more-over-the-top stressful times when we tend to give ourselves less instead of the more we

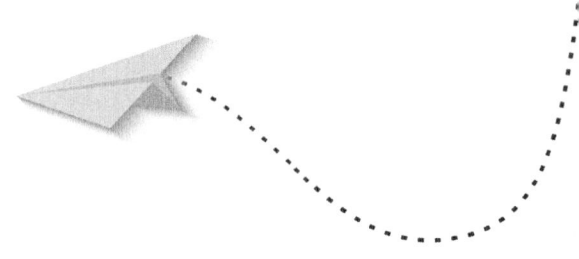

desperately need. It's a wonder I've experienced and seen many times over through students near and far. In fact, many of my students have also written on this very subject.

So, practice and test all this out for yourself. You have nothing to lose and so much to gain. Allow yourself to feel better, to have more, and to do more, and when that gets uncomfortable, and it may, practice Reiki and relax. Just because you have more doesn't mean you need to do more, but you do deserve to feel better, and you have an answer that helps you achieve that in the palm of your hands.

> *To stop is human; to begin again without self-judgement is the mark of personal growth.*

How Convenience Can Impede Practice

At one time or another, most students will stop using Reiki. This is rarely a conscious act, instead it's more of a forgetting to practice or a chore left undone due to lack of time. In most cases, the student doesn't realize they've stopped until they start to realize that they feel more stressed than usual, aren't eating well or taking care of themselves. Sometimes that acknowledgment happens in days, sometimes, it's weeks and sometimes it's years. For most, our lapse in practice starts with forgetting to practice one day, which then becomes three, and then one week or more passes. Still, lost practice can be found again, but before we get to that, let's expound on some of the reasons why we stop.

The answer isn't found in a straight line; it's more of a roundabout that encourages us to question how we define convenience and how convenience causes us to redefine what we value. Culturally, most of us have been indoctrinated into an upside-down value system when it comes to self-care. The value system is meant to support us in understanding why it's important to take care of ourselves and establish a consistent self-care regime. However, the system fails to practice what it preaches, and this often leaves us feeling conflicted by its contradictions, meaning that while it tells us one thing, it demonstrates value for its opposite. Our unspoken and underacknowledged ethos celebrates looking good over feeling good, and prizes doing for others over providing consistent quality self-care. Our personal and societal conflict stems from knowing the demands of this value system are unsustainable, if not a bit ridiculous. Still mostly unaware, we comply and conform, making choices that negatively impact our well-being and contradict what we claim we want for ourselves and others because, oddly enough, it's more convenient. And by convenient, I mean, it's easier to go with the rolling tide of society than to go against it for sake of the self. Furthermore, it's the push of that rolling tide of convenience that not only redefines our values, it creates behaviors that cause us to go against our better judgement but help us to conform with the crowd.

It's fair to say that our desire for convenience is something we often take for granted; something regarded more as the way it is and less of a choice made. In our conflict, we often defend conveniences as a necessary evil, claim them as something we're entitled to or deserving of, or plead for them as something needed until a sense of control and calm is restored. Our convenience conundrum is constructed by our value system, and if that changed, our relationship with convenience would be a healthier one. So why then, don't we consider Reiki a convenience and value it as a self-practice that improves well-being and makes a host of other things possible? The answer is, we do to some degree. It's our quieter self-preservation that gave us the motivation to receive an attunement in the first place. What's needed next is to further allow that self-preservation that moved us to deepen our self-care to help us to practice what we preach and change what we elevate in terms of convenience and use it to support sustainability.

So, if you've recently found yourself out of practice, or if it's been some time since you've used Reiki, the good news is you can start again, now, and ideally, with as little self-judgement as possible. There is no penance to pay, simply Reiki to enjoy. Consider gentle and direct daily reminders. To be effective, reminders should be cued at times that allow and encourage practice. Remember, Reiki is something that can be enjoyed in public and does not require a meditative state to enjoy, so, a cupped Reiki hand placed in your lap while waiting for public transportation or watching a match is practice. You can also start preparing for bed fifteen minutes earlier, so that you can lay down and give yourself Reiki before bed. You can do it while talking on the phone, listening to a podcast, or shopping online, to name a few instances and examples. Additionally, reconnecting with friends who practice Reiki can further support you in sustaining a daily practice, and participating in community events like Reiki Shares can convey a sense of belonging that not only encourages practice but also provides new learning opportunities.

Beyond that, there's also hope with the glimmer of change upon the horizon. While our value system and its contradictions often dominate our way of life with little escape from its influence, there is respite. More and more self-care practices are becoming more of a virtue admired than a character flaw judged. And while looking good is still and will likely always be more important to society than feeling good, more people are starting to believe you can have both. And this is a critical step towards changing our definitions of beauty to be more inclusive by valuing natural well-being and folding its glow into the language of beauty with the same regard, if not higher, than that of a top-quality makeup highlighter.

So, if you've stopped, or when you stop in the future, don't panic. You haven't failed and you can start again, even as you read the next line. It can be helpful to remember that daily practice is simply made up of a series of days, weeks, etc. that started as one instance, followed by a next and a next and a next. So, view the journey as an ultra-marathon, not as a sprint. And be kind and tempered in self-judgment, knowing you're on your side.

> *Sometimes when you've come so far, it's helpful to review where you've been.*

A Brief Review

So, we've covered a lot of material in each of these two parts. This essay then is one that you can skip if you'd like, as it's a brief recap, but I'd encourage you not to. Often, explanations are expanded on when given or said in a slightly different way that can provide new insights. To be sure, I've kept this one brief, but felt it more valuable to be included than discarded and I hope you agree. If nothing else, let this essay be a quick reference for you.

1. What is Reiki?

Reiki is the name given to two things: a specific natural energy vibration used for healing and a systematic practice created to use said healing vibration. To use Reiki, students require an attunement and some basic training. Once a student has received an attunement, that student becomes a channel for Reiki. Which means that Reiki will flow through the student's cupped hand on demand. Meaning, whenever the student wants to practice Reiki, all that is needed is for the student to place their hand in the cupped hand position and direct it toward the body.

2. How does Reiki help?

Reiki provides remedy and repair to the physical body and the aura sustained through the wear and tear of daily life. To be clear, daily life is draining, even on good days, and that is not because there is anything wrong; it's because life itself takes energy, and our lives are lived within a shared environment. To put this statement in perspective, it's also true to say that life is dehydrating, which is why hydration is also a daily activity that's required for good health and well-being.

A Reiki practice is preventative by nature; similar to the way good hydration and dental hygiene are. This means that while you may never know exactly what Reiki has saved you from, in terms of illness or injury, it's certain to help you recover from the toils of your day, much like drinking water does as well as brushing your teeth.

Reiki is restorative, provides natural relaxation and is rebalancing. Many lineages call these the three R's of Reiki, making the benefits of Reiki easier to remember. Received throughout the day, Reiki can feel energizing. Received at the end of the day, it can feel relaxing, making it both easier to get to sleep and for sleep itself to be deeper. With being better rested, relaxed and energized, greater balance will follow and you will feel better.

3. What do I do with it?

Practice, practice, practice. Unlike most self-care practices, Reiki doesn't require a large time commitment or really any time commitment. Because Reiki doesn't require a meditative state, special equipment or privacy to practice, Reiki is something you can do while doing other things — like reading this essay. While setting aside some quiet, private time to practice is a luxury worthy of having at times, it's not necessary and should not be a barrier to practice. This is an important point for students to understand because with every day that passes, lives appear to become more complex, with time becoming more limited. Knowing that a strong self-care Reiki practice doesn't add another thing to the to-do list makes it all the more likely that students will practice.

As mentioned earlier, practice begins by placing your hand in the cupped hand position. This starts the flow of Reiki. Gently placing your cupped hand anywhere on the body that feels comfortable starts your self-care treatment. You are welcome to use two hands, for double the fun, or one if that suits you or is more comfortable. Either hand will deliver Reiki, as will both. I make the point of mentioning this as an injury or weakness in one hand or arm need not leave you feeling that you can't practice. Also, it may be convenience or necessity that only one hand is used. In either case, in every case, it's enough. You are practicing Reiki.

4. Am I using it right?

If you follow the instructions provided above, the answer is yes. If you feel Reiki coming out of your hands, great. But if you don't, try not to worry. Feeling it can take time, and feeling it can mean different things to different people. The good news is, whether you feel it or not, if you are doing it as described above, you're receiving all the healthful benefits of it. It can also be helpful to keep in mind that feeling it doesn't need to mean feeling something coming out of your hands as you practice; it can be a general, gentle, all-around feeling of being more relaxed, more balanced than usual. Perhaps you feel nothing when you practice, but you notice you're sleeping better, feel more relaxed or have more energy at the end of the day or at the end of a long week. Try to keep in mind that these feelings are the true result of feeling Reiki.

Closing Thoughts

Reiki is a gift that wants for nothing. It requires no tithe or devotion and seeks no reward or recompense. Reiki holds no praise or judgment, and it doesn't become stronger or weaker based on the number of people who use it. Reiki simply is, and it offers a unique form of healing that when practiced will provide daily support to your balance and well-being. Reiki doesn't mind if you've forgotten to practice, and it is completely yielded to your authority. Reiki becomes available to you the moment you've had your attunement, but the decision to use it is entirely yours. It matters not to Reiki whether you use it, it matters to you, for it is you alone who benefits. Knowing this can take the pressure to practice right off you, for there is no room for guilt and obligation here. Add to that the knowledge that practice is your exercise of control, and you have the makings of empowerment. To that end, Reiki is a tool that empowers its practitioner with access to a new level of wellness. I mean, that alone is exciting, isn't it? In seeking an attunement, students are expressing a desire to feel better; in practicing, students are exercising the power and the control to feel it.

In speaking with people who confess that despite having a Reiki attunement, they rarely exercise the power to practice regularly, I consistently hear a lack of confidence underlying their regret or reason. A lack of confidence in practice is understandable when you consider that an afternoon or a weekend spent learning Reiki may be sufficient to complete an attunement, but it's simply not enough time to help students build the confidence needed to establish consistent practice. To do that effectively takes time, and teachers never have enough of that. Still, teachers do their best with the information they have, in the time allotted for teaching. However, limited class time coupled with the transience of most students presents real challenges for teachers hoping to help students build confidence in practice. So, to encourage more face time while adding value to students, I recommend that teachers consider offering refresher courses for currently attuned students, in addition to holding Reiki events, such as Reiki Shares.

Refresher courses succeed in two remarkably valuable ways. First, they give students more time with the course material and with practice. This gives students time to feel capable and supported in their new daily habit. Second, it helps to create community among students, who learn not only by listening to instruction, but by discussing Reiki amongst themselves in the breaks or asking questions of one another during group practice. I currently offer refresher courses for levels 1, 2 and Master. I offer these refresher courses in addition to new attunement classes and have found them an indispensable tool in supporting students create and nurture their daily practice. Refresher courses review the class curriculum and offer extended time for group practice but do not include an attunement ceremony. Students value having time to hear the teachings again, as few can retain everything that was taught the first time around. This not only enables students to deepen their understanding of what was taught in the original class, it generates excitement and commitment to practice. In short, it's an added step that helps the student build confidence. This can and often does lead to students moving on to high attunement levels, most particularly students who enjoy Reiki but didn't think they would have an interest in the higher practitioner and/or master levels.

Reiki events, such as a Reiki Share, offer open opportunities for students to invite friends who are not attuned to experience Reiki at no charge or by donation or at a lesser rate than a session would be. Reiki Healing Shares offer little in terms of group instruction and instead focus on supervised practice. It's the Reiki lab for the attunement class.

But what to do if either option isn't a possibility for you as a student? What if you've lost touch with your teacher and/or don't have a community available to spur you on? To you I say, don't worry; really, don't. With your attunement, you have everything you need in the palm of your hand. All you need to do is practice. Start by gently placing your hand in the cupped hand position and lightly lay it on your lap or anywhere comfortable. This is an exercise of empowerment in well-being. This is an act of love, of self-care, and no one needs to know you're doing it. Relax, then, and don't spend too much time thinking about it. Instead, practice and do so alongside other things. Practice gently throughout the day and into the week. Then without applying any pressure to perform, occasionally check-in with yourself to notice if you feel more rested or feel less stressed than usual. In the meantime, don't stress about building confidence; practice alone will take care of that, and the essays here will be here to support you and provide encouragement when you need it.

And with that, we naturally transition into what's next: our Part III, Answering Following-up Questions. These essays provide answers to the questions that are often asked as a result of practice.

PART III

Answering Follow-up Questions

Introduction

"**Good** question!" Those are the two most inspired words any teacher can say to a student. In my estimation, "good question" is even more inspired and encouraging than "good job." This is because "good job" follows action, and "good question" follows action + contemplation. "Good job" acknowledges a student has performed well. "Good question" acknowledges that a student has performed well, learned something as a result, and seeks to extend that learning through further questioning and discussion. "Good question" is as pure of an encouragement as any student can hope to receive. It is a road sign that tells the student they are moving in an enriching direction. It is both a call forward and a call that says make way, but perhaps what makes the statement "good question" so valuable and compelling is in its power to remind both student and teacher that a teacher's calling is one of support and guidance to those in active pursuit of learning.

Teaching is not a job that ends when class does. It is a rich and progressive purpose that calls one forward to teach. It is a call to do all that is possible to lift others up in an effort to better all lives, and that includes those who have no interest in the given course of study. This is because the role of teacher is not only fulfilled in providing the particulars of any given subject. It is also fulfilled in inspiring and guiding others in the pursuit of knowledge itself. It is in that spirit and in the desire to encourage students to keep asking questions that this next section is written.

The title of this section, Part III, Answering Follow-up Questions may, at first, seem unexpected if not a bit confusing. So, let's clarify what is meant here by answering, what is a follow-up question? A follow-up question is a question that develops as a direct result of practice. These aren't first-tier questions. First-tier questions come as a result of learning something new. Examples are what Reiki is, or how to practice. These are second-tier questions. Second-tier questions come as a result of practice. If you are like most students, you are bound to find that practice has a wonderful tendency to inspire questions. This is because dedicated practice often results in a heightened level of personal awareness. What I describe here is a heightened awareness of how Reiki is affecting you and how you feel about Reiki and the changes it's helping you to make. Acknowledging changes and noticing differences achieved through practice are common examples of this heightened awareness and are often the precursors to follow-up questions. Therefore, this section highlights some of the more common follow-up questions I've received from students. Questions like: Why do I feel insecure sometimes with Reiki, and how can I become more comfortable with it? Why isn't Reiki alleviating all my symptoms? And, it's been a long time since I've practiced, have I lost Reiki and need to be reattuned?

These, as well as the other questions included in this section are all good questions. I've included them here because I have been asked these questions many times over and have consistently found that exploring the answers to these questions help students deepen their relationship to Reiki and help them develop greater confidence in practice. To that end, and I'll say it bluntly: I've found that providing useable explanations and answers to these good questions have consistently made the difference between a student practicing each day or falling off the habit altogether.

Additionally, my hope is that by going into the deeper cuts of follow-up questions, that it encourages our larger Reiki community to expand its conversations on the subject, so that we are not only actively seeking to provide answers to the questions we can answer, but that we can start to take aim at providing clear, useable answers to the questions we currently don't have answers to. Questions that delve deeper into the how's and why's of Reiki and wellness. In that spirit, honoring our practice by allowing our follow-up questions to lead the way can be our start to expanding our conversations and adding depth to understanding of the subject.

To be clear, this is not an FAQ (frequently asked question) section. FAQs in Reiki are readily available and easy to find. Besides, the first two sections of this book do a lot to both directly and indirectly address FAQs. This section is meant only to address the follow-up questions students engaged in daily practice tend to ask. Questions that expose their hopes and fears in Reiki. Questions that dare to test the limits of Reiki, and questions that help students refine their language, so they have greater confidence both in practice and in speaking about Reiki to others. Like steps on a ladder, follow-up questions guide the student in their ascent to higher learning. This is of value because true progression, the process of moving towards an advanced state, follows dedicated practice. Be it in sport, in mastering the manipulation of a musical instrument or redesigning the way cars work today, it is through practice, through kinesthetic learning, feeling, that we are inspired to ask follow-up questions that guide us to our next steps in learning our chosen field. It is through that curiosity and effort that we gain the ability and the confidence needed to take what we've learned and progress it to the next level of understanding.

The answers are written in celebration of those questions and in an effort to continue to encourage students at all levels to keep asking. They are written with admiration for the student's journey and in reverence and support of the teacher's purpose. My hope is that this section provides some of that support, for each of you represent the light leading the way. These essays are also written in the hope that one day some of these students will be inspired to become teachers and take part in teaching future generations of practitioners. So, with that in mind, and with a desire to know what's next to understand and explore, let the questioning begin.

Student statement & follow-up question:

"I love learning Reiki but sometimes I feel unsure. Why do I feel insecure sometimes with Reiki, and how can I become more comfortable with it?"

How Do I Become More Comfortable With Reiki?

When students talk about feeling insecure with Reiki, it's almost exclusively in the context of what they *are* or *aren't* feeling. If they feel something, they want to know — Is that it? If they don't feel something, they want to know — Is it working? And when that question is answered (it is working) they want to know: If it's working (which it is), why can't I feel anything?

Does any of this sound familiar? If it does, you're in good company. At least initially, when students speak of feeling unsure about Reiki, that insecurity is rooted in feeling it. But before we can really dig in to feeling as it relates to Reiki, it's valuable to understand our relationship to feeling as a whole because, for the most part, most people, most of the time, are unsure, if not uncomfortable with what they feel — whether that's Reiki or other things.

To be clear, when it comes to feeling, thinking appears to be the preferred and more acceptable alternative. We have been taught to value thinking over feeling when it comes to learning. Our primary, secondary and higher educational systems are built on and reinforce those values. Moreover, thinking appears more tangible than feeling and so is considered more reliable. However, I posit that that is not altogether accurate, or perhaps it's more precise to say that while it is true for certain types of learning, such as physical, immediate perceivable and measurable things, it is not true for more subtle, nuanced studies. In fact, it could be argued that even in the learning of the physically perceivable, mastery is achieved when the student goes beyond the mental confines of how, to the immersion into feeling.

This mastery, of course, is in almost all cases the result of practice. Driving a car presents an example of this. New drivers learn how to drive by learning what the traffic laws are and what equipment is used. This is a mental exercise. But when it comes to actual driving, most drivers will say, it all comes down to feeling. This is a bodily exercise. How the car feels, how the road feels and how confident the driver feels driving on crowded roads make new drivers become experienced drivers through practice.

This is not at all meant to make a case that one form of learning is superior to another. In fact, quite the opposite. Both are necessary, both are valuable. It's simply to point out that despite both styles of learning being necessary, most of us are trained to trust one form over another, instead of seeing them as two equally effective tools in the toolbox of learning. When we do that, one form will give us confidence and one will leave us feeling unsure, which brings us back to the student's concern and her question.

There really isn't much thinking required in Reiki, making it unlike most things you'll learn. In Reiki, you learn using the parts of you that feel, not the parts you use that think. The mind, while necessary to get you to class, isn't the star player once in class. The reason for this is there are simply aspects of the practice that are not immediately observable, and since the mind's job is to observe and measure things, it's often insecure with an intangible like Reiki. The lack of thinking required or, better said, the absence of its role in learning Reiki, can feel a bit unnerving and may cause some to doubt their ability to learn this way. But to help quell this self-doubt, I offer a dash of clarity and a heap of encouragement. I offer these to highlight how you unknowingly use that feeling part you of all the time, because getting comfortable learning through the feeling part of you can help make you unstoppable in your pursuit of Reiki.

To begin, a dash of clarity. Sure, Reiki is intangible, but then again some of the very best things in life are. Love is intangible, as is your gut feeling, and I'm sure both have saved you on more than one occasion. Self-doubt is also intangible, and if you're like most people, then on more than one occasion, it's gotten in your way. Jealously, hope, chi, luck, faith — all intangible, and much of our lives are influenced and guided by intangibles, and to be fair, we find great comfort and security in that.

Now, you might have noticed that many of the things I've just described as intangibles could be called something else: feelings. Inspiration, creativity, insecurity, fear — can you imagine a life without them? Would you want to? For what we call intangibles often give us a sense of being part of something greater than ourselves.

So then, how do we use this dash of clarity to comfort us in the moments our mind feels insecure learning and practicing Reiki? I suggest we start at the beginning, and further build our confidence by seeing that we already use feeling more than we think we do, so not only have we nothing to fear, we have a heap of encouragement coming. And here it is.

When learning things by feeling and then by doing, we're engaged in kinetic learning. Reiki is best learned this way. So is playing the guitar, but unlike playing the guitar, with Reiki you can't rely on sound to tell you how you're doing. Reiki is a vibration that is more subtle. This feeling, because it is a subtle experience, may be hard to describe. What's good to remember is that it's not the description of what is felt but the feeling taking place that is valuable. And for some, being aware of feeling, that is to say, being aware of what one is feeling, can take time and there is no need to rush. Rushing will only impede the learning process. In this way, patience and trust are your best learning aids. Patience to give you time, and trust to help quell any fear that may come up. To be fair, most people are a little spooked by things they can sense and feel but can't see.

Without a doubt, there will be students who won't feel anything initially, and if you are one of those students, I say to you reassuringly — don't worry. You're not broken or inept when it comes to Reiki — not in the least. Furthermore, Reiki doesn't require you to feel a thing. Reiki works whether you feel it or not. So, please, place no pressure on yourself to feel it; instead, relax and keep reading, because a few things mentioned here might surprise you.

When it comes to feeling, the truth is, our days are guided as much by feeling as by thought. Without realizing it, we're feeling all the time, but more notably, we're also trusting those feelings and using them to our benefit. This is reflective in our expressions, in our behavior and in our choices. We spend our days expressing our feelings when we say, we feel good, tired, sick, hungry, or thirsty. We rarely question these feelings. We may say, "I think I'm tired," or "I think I'm hungry," but we still often respond to that point more than we dismiss it. Our behavior is influenced by the impatience we feel waiting for the kettle to boil or at a stoplight when we are feeling pressure to be somewhere else. Our desires for things to change and our wishes for time to stand still or hurry up come from feeling. Our feelings often portend our behavior or a condition like, "I feel like dancing," or "I feel like I'm coming down with something." Again, in either instance, we trust the sentiment more than we don't, and we act on it more than we push it away. Furthermore, and in both instances, upon hearing someone share this, we immediately know what that person means because we know and have had the same feeling at one point or another.

We see other examples of the use of feeling in much of our choices. Choices like what we wear or what we eat. Generally, people dress how they feel. Even when given a dress-code to abide, people will generally make choices within the code that express how they feel. People will often express feeling when choosing a meal. They will say things like "I feel like I want something spicy," or "I feel like I want fries today." The music we choose to listen to is also, more often than it's not, an expression of how we feel. This is also often true of the people we choose to spend time with, the shows we choose to watch, the games we choose to play. Choices such as these are usually the result of what we felt like doing at the time, and we do so trusting those feelings.

Feeling is something we all use and depend upon. This means that as a teacher, I find my work is less about encouraging students to feel, with underlying inference being that there is a lack of feeling going on, and more about reminding students that feelings are ubiquitous. So much so, that we not only fail to recognize their place within our daily lives, but we take for granted how we much we trust them to enrich our lives. With this gentle reminder, students can expand their confidence when it comes to feeling to include this way of learning Reiki. This not only helps; it has the potential of helping the student better define what it means to feel it.

So many students fear they can't feel Reiki because there is an expectation that when they place their hand in the cupped position, a sensation should follow. And to be fair, for some, a sensation does follow, but that alone is not feeling Reiki, so is not the singular benchmark or measurement for knowing it. Moreover, confidence in Reiki really starts when the student accepts that it was a feeling that brought them to class in the first place. From there, it blossoms, and I'll provide an illustration of that point.

After a group practice, one of my students, Riza, said that when he gave Reiki to different students, the Reiki felt different to him. I said that difference you felt was real, but it wasn't Reiki that felt different. Then I said, "See, I'll show you."

I asked who he had given Reiki to and asked each of them how it felt to them. Both students said they felt great, relaxed; one even said that she loved how gentle he was. The point was, both students recounted very similar experiences, experiences that are common to Reiki.

He was so relieved. He actually feared that he may have done something wrong.

I said, "No, you didn't do anything wrong. You can't interfere with Reiki or change it in any way."

What he felt when he practiced was the difference of the two individual students he worked on and confused that for Reiki, since he was standing over them to give them Reiki. This is so common, it's a question that almost always comes up at a Reiki Share. I also gently pointed out that neither of the two students described their experience of receiving Reiki in terms of how Reiki, the vibration, felt to them, things like, "I felt heat or energy." Their responses were grounded on feeling the remedy Reiki brought to them. It was a wonderful learning moment for everyone involved. I guess you could say, it was an ah-ha moment.

In summary, the insecurities students feel in a Reiki class are natural and nothing to shy away from. In fact, sometimes students can confuse insecurity or nervousness with excitement. Reiki can be thrilling. To think that you have become attuned to a healing vibration that you can use to care for yourself is nothing short of a wonder to behold, and the experience and the potency of its power is yours to use and enjoy. I encourage all students to lean into that feeling and allow it to help you heal, and to remind you that your abilities to learn and grow are aided by the mind, but are not limited to it.

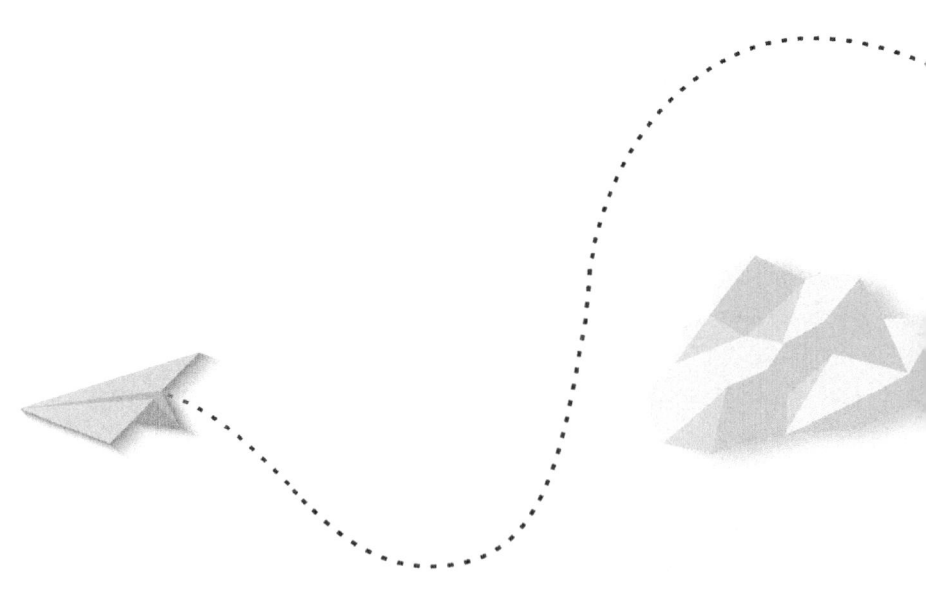

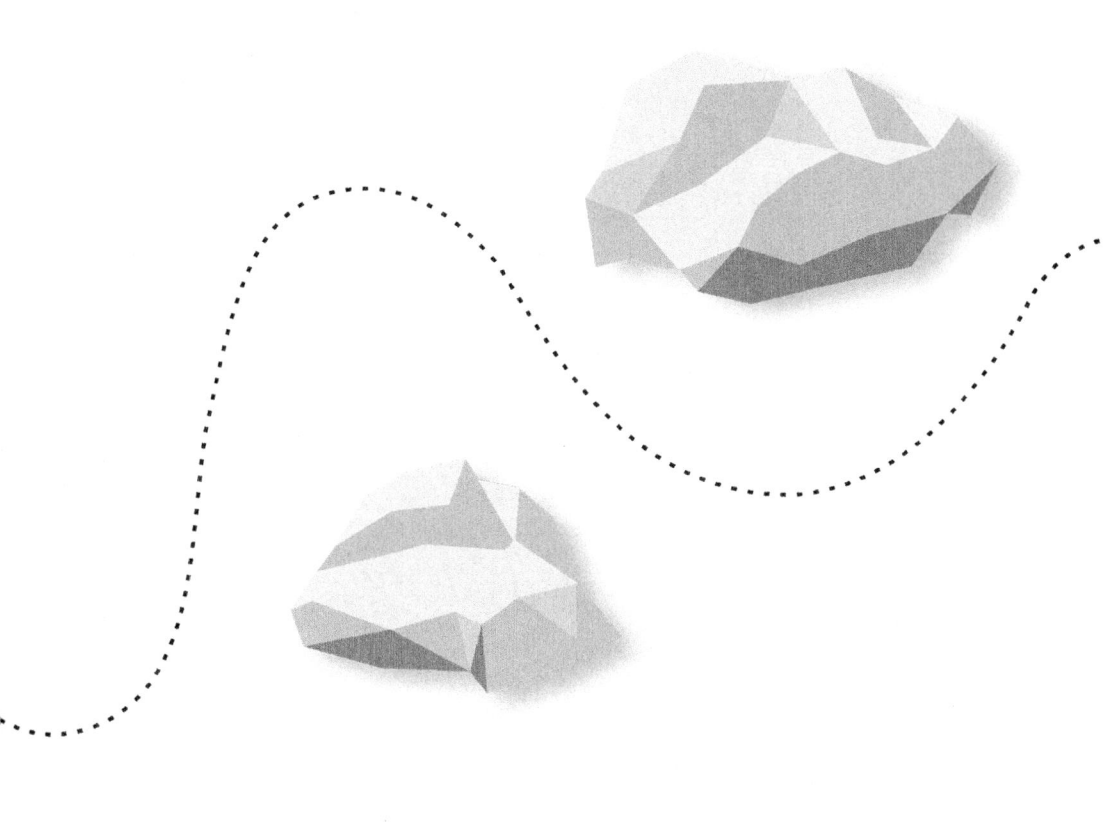

Student statement & follow-up question:

"The feeling of Reiki in my hand has changed. Why has the feeling changed? Why don't I feel my Reiki anymore, or why is it less intense?"

Why Don't I Feel my Reiki Anymore, or Why is it Less Intense?

To be clear, this question is always in regard to the feeling that some students experience coming through the cupped Reiki hand, not the feeling that follows practice. The answer then focuses on changes to that sensation. To provide a complete answer, I start by discussing feeling in terms of personal experience before moving into how feelings naturally change over time.

When describing the feeling of rain on your face, there is consensus of what that feels like. Descriptions may differ slightly, but most will include some description of wetness. The feeling of rain upon the skin is both easily distinguished and easily agreed upon. The thing is, not all things feel universal or enjoy a consensus among people. Of course, there are obvious examples to the contrary, rain on the skin being one, but for the most part feeling is subjective.

What we describe when we feel is based on a vocabulary given to us by others since birth. This vocabulary is meant to provide more than a shared language, it attempts to unite people through agreement. It hopes to provide a target for people to aim for in describing things, including what is felt.

In many ways, it's successful in its attempt to draw consensus among a group, but this also has a downside when it comes to feeling. That downside is that these targets inadvertently create expectations, and when expectations are not met, worry, distress and fear usually follow. Worry, distress and fear are impediments to feeling and stop us from engaging with our experiences. What can help provide remedy to worry, distress and fear is the reminder that ultimately, any target on feeling is a moving target and not only can we expect to see differences among descriptions, we do so on a daily basis. While as humans we find comfort in a tribe, we are also individuals and our experiences, while at times may be shared, are always personal.

For example, one person's favorite song can be described as the bane of all music by another. Is either person wrong, or is it simply that the feeling the song engenders is not the same for all who listen? Sometimes a hug can offer the most comforting feeling, and then another time, the same hug from the same person on a different day can feel imposing. Wind in one moment can feel refreshing and at a turn becomes relentless. What we feel is in constant flux because we are in constant flux, as is the world we inhabit.

While our collective habit is to focus on changes to our outer environment over our inner environment, I encourage students when it comes to Reiki to always start by looking inward. While it provides the same benefits to all, Reiki is uniquely experienced. To this end, I tell all my students that there is no wrong answer when describing what you feel through your hands when practicing Reiki, with one exception: pain.

Reiki is natural and healing the same way water is, and like water, if a person has a problem with it or finds it distressing, uncomfortable or painful, that highlights an underlying issue that requires attention. Such cases are rare. I have only seen one such case in regard to Reiki, and it was the result of an incomplete attunement. Once the problem was identified by the student, the teacher assessed the issued, found the cause and reattuned the student. The problem was then solved, and Reiki flowed unimpeded and without any discomfort. If you or anyone you know experiences such an instance, which again, is very rare, so rare in fact that I've only seen one, then your teacher can help and is there to be your first resource for support.

Aside from that, Reiki can feel like almost anything coming through the hand. It can also feel like nothing. Nothing is an acceptable description for what Reiki feels like. That, along with heat, a general warmth, a buzzing feeling, tingling, humming, pulse or flow of energy. Any and all work to describe the feeling of Reiki, and that is because the feeling of Reiki is as personal as its description.

If a student asks me if Reiki feels like heat or humming or something else, I say, "There is not one description for Reiki; if you're feeling something, that's great, enjoy it." If a student tells me he or she doesn't feel something through the hand when practicing, I say, "That's fine, feeling it through the hand is not required for it to work." But what if you do feel Reiki coming through your hand, and that feeling changes over time or dissipates and disappears? Is this something to worry about? No, not at all. Change is natural and to be expected. This is especially true the more you practice.

Humans are pattern seekers, which means that we tend to lean on past experiences to make sense of our present. Using past patterns helps us to set expectations. But again, this is a moving target, because as humans, we are always changing and adapting to new circumstances, situations and environments. This means our baseline for comparison is also always changing. You see, the more your practice, the more you will become accustomed to the feeling coming through your hand, and the more accustomed you become, the more you adapt to the change and it simply becomes your new normal. This can be likened to people who live near an active railroad track or close to an airport. Often these residents cease hearing the sounds of the engines as the trains or planes pass. It's only when a visitor stops in and asked about it that the resident acknowledges the sound, and usually with a bit of a laugh. Does that mean the engines have suddenly become quieter, or has the resident simply adjusted to the sound to such an extent that she no longer hears it? Clearly, it's the latter, and this type of example can provide comfort to those who experience changes in the feeling, for it's a gentle reminder that it's not Reiki that changes, it's you that adapts and your perception that's changed.

So, while it may be enjoyable to feel Reiki flowing through your hand, if these feelings change or if you suddenly notice you don't feel it through your hand anymore, it's nothing to worry about. In fact, it can be seen as a natural transition for students with a dedicated practice. The more you use Reiki, the more you will become accustomed to its feel, and the more that happens, the less of it you're likely to feel because the feeling is no longer new. Instead, it's become your new normal, and that means you're consistently receiving better self-care.

In addition, this change also provides a new opportunity for the student to change their point of view and description of feeling Reiki. This is a change away from feeling Reiki coming through the hand and towards feeling how Reiki helps to support you and your well-being. It then becomes more of a bodily feeling, a feeling-into the results of daily practice. To be sure, descriptions here also vary, but they tend to revolve among the common descriptors of feeling more relaxed and/or feeling less depleted at the end of the day. The advantage of opening up one's perspective to focus on the benefits experienced as a result of practice is that it can make practice more fulfilling.

So, if you're a student who feels something of a sensation through their cupped hand during practice I say, enjoy the feeling of today, and worry not if it changes tomorrow. If you feel a focus on feeling is necessary when you practice, consider placing your focus on the feeling that follows practice, and if you feel no focus is necessary that's great, too. To be honest, the only necessity in Reiki is practice, so do that and enjoy.

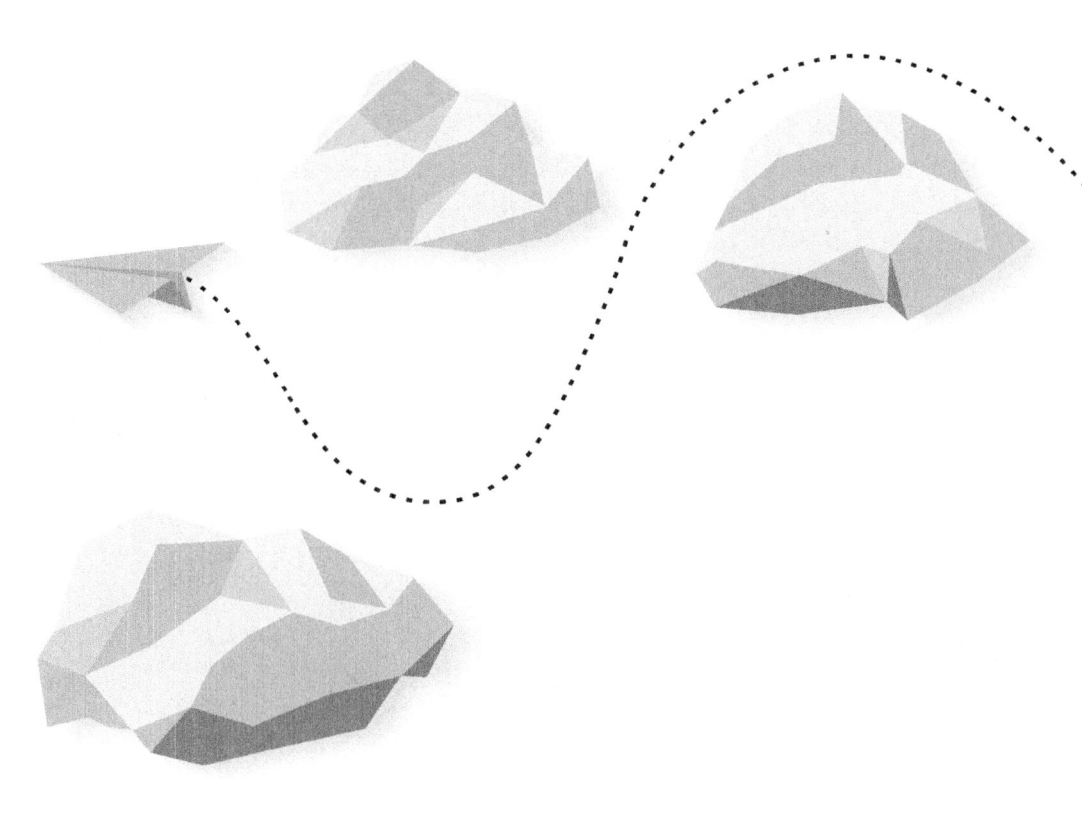

Student statement & follow-up question:

"I learned Reiki to help me relax, but I don't feel anything when I practice. Does this mean my Reiki doesn't work for me? If I don't feel Reiki, how do I know it is working?"

If I Don't Feel Reiki, How Do I Know That it's Working?

This is such a good question and one I get frequently. The key in knowing that Reiki is working is not found in the sensation a student feels when practicing, it is found in the feeling a student experiences following practice. When a student states they don't feel Reiki, they're generally describing a lack of feeling in one of the three areas: coming from their hand during practice, being felt at the site where Reiki is being delivered, being felt through the body, like a buzzing or a form of heat. This lack of feeling is the result of an expectation not being met, and it is not a statement of a student's ability to feel or work with energy.

Generally speaking, when a student makes this statement, it's usually the result of comparing their experience with that of another student. Sometimes, that comparison can even come from an eager teacher wanting their students to have an experience and so urging students to feel something and share with the group. However, as mentioned before, feeling something when practicing is not necessary and it's not a requirement for practice. If you feel something, that's great, and I encourage you to enjoy while it lasts; but if you don't feel something, don't worry. I mention this a few times because these issues are so common, and this question, if it goes unanswered or is misunderstood, will lead a student to stop practicing. So, assurances that as long as you're practicing, you're doing just fine are valuable because they help the student feel confident by lending them a compass when they feel a bit lost. For this reason, I again advise students not to focus on "feeling it" when they are practicing because it inadvertently places pressure and expectation on practice. Instead, I encourage students to relax and to take off the pressure that they should be feeling something during practice.

This calls for the student to shift their focus away from trying to feel sensation and to becoming aware of its benefits. The reasons I encourage this shift away from focusing on sensation is that initial sensations, like those mentioned above, are not instructive. Meaning, those sensations will not help you learn Reiki, understand its benefits, or the need for practice. What is instructive, however, is the feeling that *follows* practice — what we call feeling better — more relaxed, balanced, energized. Put simply, the benefits of practice. These feelings are instructive because these feelings describe the benefits of practice, and that is why I encourage my students to place their attention there. These feelings are also goals, and they'll be the reason you will come back to practice if you've taken a break at some point or forgot to practice. But don't take my word for it — if you're feeling a bit insecure about it or skeptical, I encourage you test it out yourself. If you haven't already started, you can start now.

For many students, the 21-day adjustment period following a Reiki attunement is the student's first opportunity to test this out. If you haven't had the opportunity of a 21-adjustment period, I'll explain it briefly. A 21-day adjustment period is the period of daily practice that follows an attunement class. Your first day of the 21-day adjustment period begins the following day and is designed to teach students the benefits of Reiki through practice. During this time, students are directed to practice on themselves for at least 15 minutes each day for 21 consecutive days. If, however, you're a student who was not assigned or has not completed a 21-day adjustment period following their attunement, there is no reason why you couldn't start a 21-day adjustment period now. All that is required is a personal commitment to practice each day for 21 consecutive days for at least 15 minutes. Ideally, those minutes are done at one time each day, but while that is the preferred method, it's not a requirement. Better you practice in increments than to not practice because you can't do it all in one go. For example, I prefer to do mine before bed, but it can be done in smaller increments of time throughout the day if and when necessary. The result of practice, in other words, the feeling that follows regular practice, is the benefit of practice. Don't worry about checking in with how you feel immediately following practice. That's not really how it works, either; instead, practice and relax, and let the feeling reveal itself to you when it comes naturally. It's likely to pleasantly surprise you, like it did to the student in the case below.

I was speaking to one of my students, who is also a teacher. Her name is Debbie and she shared with me the story of one of her recently attuned students, Corinne. In short, Corinne came to Reiki as a last resort. She was irritable and uncomfortable most of the time. She was consistently experiencing high levels of stress that left her feeling drained by the end of the day. Her fatigue would grow throughout the week to the point where she was unable to do anything but recover over her weekend. Corinne enjoyed her class and the attunement, but she didn't feel Reiki the way she believed the other students did. Still, she was a hopeful skeptic with a deep desire to feel better and a willingness to have a go.

As instructed, she committed herself to the 21-day adjustment period assigned to her by Debbie at the end of class. Corinne reported back that starting her 21-day adjustment period practice was hard at first. This was because she didn't think she felt anything, so it was hard to justify why she was doing it. She felt a bit silly and mostly stupid, but she had faith in her teacher, who encouraged her to continue even if she didn't feel anything. Reluctantly, she did.

She practiced each day, and by the end of her first week, much to her surprise and relief, she noticed she wasn't exhausted. In fact, she felt good and was looking forward to a weekend not spent in bed or stuck languishing on the couch. This for her was a revelation that gave her a sense of freedom she feared had long been lost. She was now a hopeful skeptic suddenly without conflict. These realizations felt life-changing. Reiki did what she was told it would, and she felt better even if she was still unsure if she felt anything in practice. What was clear was that now she knew for herself, Reiki works, and you don't have to feel it (sensation-wise), to feel it (benefit-wise)!

Her story is a rather common one in Reiki. In fact, when I started, I was one of those students who didn't feel anything, and it stalled my practice for a while. It wasn't until I needed help sleeping that I started practicing again. Back then, I made it a habit of falling asleep with cupped hands on my chest. I hadn't intended to do that, but that was how effective Reiki was in helping me sleep. Before I knew it, I was out. My sleep was deeper, and I woke up feeling more rested and ready for the day. From there, my practice grew, and with it my interest in Reiki. My interest grew into fascination and deep study. From there, I developed a drive for mastery, and over time that mastery brought me a desire to teach.

What became clear to me back when I was falling asleep with cupped hands on my chest is that Reiki works, and it asks for nothing from you, including your validation. Over the years, I have found the same to be true many times over in the faces and stories of so many others. Reiki, like many remarkable things, works regardless of whether you feel some kind of sensation when you engage with it. The same is true of water, which will make things wet regardless of your personal ability to feel moisture. The same can be said of gravity, which will hold you to the earth's surface regardless of whether or not you are consciously aware of its pull.

When it comes to Reiki, daily practice is all that is required to benefit from Reiki and feel better. Practice, nothing more, but certainly, nothing less.

Student statement & follow-up question:

"Reiki helped my sister sleep better. I was desperate for this to work for me, but it didn't. Why did it work for her but not for me?"

Why didn't Reiki alleviate all my Symptoms?

Reiki works all the time, but Reiki does not work on all things. This is true in the same way that water, when drunk, will always hydrate you, but it won't heal your broken toe. The difference in this example is, you don't expect water to heal your broken toe. But because Reiki has often been misrepresented and misunderstood when it comes to energy healing, many have expected it to heal everything, and these people found themselves disappointed in Reiki or filled with self-doubt about their own healing abilities when it hasn't. So, let's review what Reiki does work on and what it doesn't, and use that to understand when more is needed.

In short, Reiki is a healing practice that promotes well-being. It does this by providing repair and remedy to the daily wear and tear experienced in the physical body and the aura. Reiki does not heal trauma; it does not provide repair to injury; it does not heal acute or chronic illness; and it does not heal issues associated with karma. Reiki also doesn't work on the meridian system (an energy system that runs through body) or work directly on the mind. To be clear, this is not an exhaustive list, and it's not meant to be. Instead, it's meant to help show the limitations of Reiki as a means of better understanding it.

However, before we go any further, let me be very clear — in instances where Reiki is not providing relief of symptoms, I urge you to seek other forms of treatment. See your doctor, your acupuncturist, your therapist, or whoever you feel is best equipped to provide support and treatment for the symptom you are experiencing.

And please remember in instances such as these, Reiki hasn't failed you. But Reiki has limitations, and by understanding those, we can start to see Reiki as a tool within our wellness toolbox instead of depending on it as a cure-all. Because when we start doing that, we get better at getting ourselves what we need to help us heal.

To better understand the limitations of Reiki, I'll present two examples where symptoms experienced in two different students appear the same, but one person found remedy through Reiki while the other didn't. In our first example, two different people, Ramon and Vivienne, report experiencing sleep issues. Both use Reiki, but only Ramon reports a significant improvement in the quality of his sleep, while Vivienne reports no change. To be sure, both have benefited from using Reiki, even though only Ramon experienced better sleep. The reason why Reiki didn't help Vivienne's sleep issue is because her sleep issue is not the result of daily wear and tear. Examples of things that could cause this issue other than wear and tear include trauma or illness (both known and unknown), as well as something like hormonal or chi imbalances, neither of which are issues Reiki can remedy. Vivienne is advised to continue using Reiki to keep receiving its benefits but not depend on it as a means to correct her sleep issue. For that, she is best advised to seek another, additional form of treatment. To put this in perspective, let's compare this to an example of two people having bad breath. Both people brush, use an antiseptic mouth wash and start flossing. One person sees immediate improvement, but the second does not. This doesn't mean that the second person should stop brushing her teeth, using antiseptic mouthwash or flossing, it merely suggests that more is needed. In the second case, perhaps a digestive issue is the cause for the bad breath.

With that said, in many instances, Reiki will aid in expediting healing of more complex needs, and it may help to provide relief from the acuteness of a symptom. This is a great first step in the healing process, but again, if you're experiencing improvement but not complete remedy within a week, I encourage you to consider seeking further treatment. What follows is an example to help illustrate this point. A colleague of mine, who is also a Reiki teacher named Elliot, had a client who initially came in for Reiki. The client, named Amanda, was new to energy healing, so for her, this was a good place to start. Amanda came in looking for help for anxiety. Following a few Reiki sessions, Amanda reported back that her anxiety had changed remarkably and that she was sleeping better and felt more at ease. Amanda was very happy with this but was still struggling in some of the other aspects of her anxiety. In this example, the reason Amanda found some relief was because the wear and tear she was experiencing each day was adding to and exacerbating an underlying anxiety caused by a previous traumatic experience that she could acknowledge but was not ready to engage with in any meaningful way. By providing remedy and repair to her wear and tear, Amanda felt so much better, and in fact, her sleep improved greatly. However, this also made her underlying anxiety more apparent, and Reiki, while helpful, is not the tool to address those other underlying issues. At this point, it would be ideal for Amanda to learn Reiki, or to continue to receive regular Reiki sessions for the wear and tear and seek another solution, when she is ready, to heal the underlying anxiety.

To be sure, situations like these can be difficult to parse out initially, but with practice and patience, you can know for yourself what symptoms respond to Reiki and which issues will need another form of healing because they are not the result of daily wear and tear. In this pursuit, it's helpful to remember that understanding Reiki is not only about being able to answer what Reiki is but also about understanding its limitations. That way, you can ensure that Reiki becomes an effective healing tool that is used regularly with reverence and understanding but is not the sole tool in your wellness toolbox.

Student statement & follow-up question:

"It's been years since I've been attuned, and I never practice. Do I lose Reiki if I fail to use it?"

Do I lose Reiki if I fail to use it?

Unlike some of the previous questions asked, this one is very straightforward. No, you will not lose Reiki if you don't use it. When you were attuned to Reiki, you became a channel for it. Neither time nor non-use will close the channel. Once the channel is made, it remains open, so you will never lose access to Reiki. With that said, if you haven't used it in a long time, you may feel wary of using it, but that is more an emotional hesitation than one caused by any impingement to the channel itself. If you would like to start using Reiki again, you can start anytime by cupping your hand and placing it gently anywhere on your body. However, if you feel unsure or would simply like support, you can take a local refresher course on Reiki as a means to help you feel confident in practice once again.

Student statement & follow-up question:

"I don't understand the Reiki attunement levels. If I get more attunements, does my Reiki get stronger?"

Understanding the Attunement Levels of Reiki

The body of Reiki instruction is parceled out and taught in levels that are designed to take the student from novice to practitioner, from practitioner to Master, and support the Master in becoming a Teacher. That's only four levels in teaching the body of knowledge for Reiki. For this reason, the levels are experienced more as steep slopes than gentle transitions. Meaning that each level, while adding to the instruction provided in the last, can feel like a quantum leap.

To be sure, what follows is not based on a uniform method of defining attunement levels because there is no such method. Different lineages and teachers, sometimes within the same lineage, may offer compressed attunement levels, like teaching levels 1 & 2 together over the course of a weekend, or merging levels 3 & 4 as one Master teacher level. Or, they might offer expanded levels that take the four mentioned here and expand that information to ten or more levels. Still, the intent of this body of knowledge is relatively standard across all. But I will also acknowledge that often what is taught at the individual level differs across lineages because things like cultural influences, well-intentioned misinterpretations of past teachings, as well as personal preferences have been added over time. Therefore, what follows is an explanation of how I teach and delineate the levels. Still, the information provided is general enough to be useful in setting expectations for students across lineages and among attunement levels.

The question I receive most from students contemplating pursuit of the next level is, "Will the next level boost or make my Reiki better or greater?" The simple answer to that question is no. Once a student receives an attunement at level 1, that student becomes a channel for Reiki. Advanced attunements do not alter the channel. Your Reiki doesn't change in advanced levels. What changes is your relationship to Reiki; what deepens is your understanding of it.

So then, why are there attunements given at each level? Attunements given at levels above level 1 are providing the energetic information that class will support. The body receives the energetic information, and then your teacher provides the oral instruction that helps the mind reconcile that information. Together they are meant to help the student transform what's been received and taught into a deeper personal knowledge. Reiki is a healing practice that promotes well-being. The deeper your understanding of it, the deeper your understanding of well-being as a whole and what is needed to maximize it.

LEVEL 1 — Self-care

Level 1 is Reiki's introductory class and is the student's induction into its practice. Students are given instruction about Reiki (the vibration), receive an attunement designed to make the student a channel for Reiki to flow through and then given instruction about Reiki (the formalized healing practice), as well as the opportunity for direct experience practicing it. Students can expect to leave the course feeling renewed and personally empowered with a new practice. Through the combination of instruction and direct experience, students experience for themselves what's been missing in their daily self-care regime and come away with a new appreciation of what it means to be well.

Reiki level 1 classes are generally taught over the course of one day, so there's not a lot of time and much to accomplish. The day will consist of classroom type-instruction, an attunement ceremony, and practice where the student, now attuned, learns how to use Reiki. The key to aiding students in learning is to keep instruction simple, use plain language throughout and provide lots of relatable examples. Teaching goals of level 1 are twofold: to establish value for Reiki, and to instill confidence in the student for using this new practice. Everything the teacher will do throughout the day is working to accomplish both goals.

Students completing this level are said to have a Reiki attunement. No formal title is given. Attuned students are expected to begin incorporating Reiki into their daily self-care regime and, while permitted to give Reiki to friends and family, are not trained to see people professionally or charge for Reiki services.

LEVEL 2 — Practitioner

This level provides a broader examination of Reiki. Through its course, the student goes from apprentice to becoming an advocate for Reiki. This is known as the practitioner level, and students who complete this level are given the title Reiki practitioner, as well as bestowed the privilege of becoming a Reiki professional by seeing clients and charging money for formal Reiki sessions.

The goal of this level is that students leave the course feeling excited and enriched by their knowledge of Reiki, how it fits into the larger body of natural healing, and in their ability to speak about

Reiki and share Reiki with others in both formal and informal environments. A practitioner is an advocate for Reiki and has the choice to become a Reiki professional: someone who charges money for Reiki services, but by virtue of being a practitioner, is always and foremost an advocate. In advocacy, the practitioner is learning to speak fluently and with ease about Reiki. The practitioner is able to discuss Reiki and provide a confident answer to the question, what is Reiki, as well as dispel some of the misconceptions about Reiki by being able to confidently discuss its benefits as well as its limitations.

Students generally come to a level 2 attunement as a result of having a strong, consistent self-care practice. This practice has created positive changes in the quality of life of the student, and so the student is called to seek out more information about this incredible healing practice. Some students will come having already found a desire to work professionally in Reiki, but not all. That is an individual decision and one that is open to change. What all students share, however, is the desire for more information and to deepen their understanding of Reiki.

The teaching goals of level 2 are to gently and effectively nurture the student's confidence of practice through a blossoming reverence of Reiki, so that both may lay the foundation for advocacy and a professional practice. The teacher accomplishes her goals by providing clear instruction with temperance and providing time for questions and tangents that come up during instruction. And, as always, this must be done while helping each student build upon the confidence gained at level 1, so that the apprentice can successfully transition into an advocate who is learning how to be confident working on others and answering questions asked by clients and other inquiring minds.

Upon completion of level 2, the student comes away with a wealth of information that will take some time to digest. The course is taught over a two-day period and, like level 1, includes classroom instruction, an attunement ceremony, and practice. To be fair, students will need to hear this information multiple times before the information given fully integrates and becomes knowledge. Letting the students know this helps them to set expectations for themselves.

For this reason, I offer review courses of the level 2 curriculum for my practitioner students. Those classes do not include an attunement, since the practitioner has already received the level 2 attunement. I offer these classes at a discount relative to the original course that includes the attunement. My practitioners find it invaluable to hear the level 2 curriculum again.

Level 3 — Master

The Master's level is a rite of passage one takes from being a practitioner to becoming a Master. It's a journey of personal responsibility. The road of Mastery is paved with competence but incomplete without enthusiasm and sobriety. A love of the game, if you will, is a necessary component for the practitioner seeking mastery. Part of mastery is the willingness to face the inconvenient truth that it's not enough to know what is good for you; being a Master means living it and having the fortitude necessary to do it. Without such a personal commitment, in time, complacency erodes one's sense of purpose, derides one's sense of direction, and ground gained through learning and practice becomes lost. I realize that may sound quite serious, but it's not serious so much as it is a test of personal responsibility. To be sure, there are no shortage of Reiki Masters out there, but most of them are in title only. Mastery takes time and a commitment to practice.

The teaching goals at this level shift from one of pure instruction to one of instruction and advanced mentoring. The teacher, who was once seen as instructor and role model, now becomes instructor, guide and role model. The teacher moves beyond simply providing instruction to helping the student bring forward what they know and to find within themselves the personal commitment to practice each day, and to find within that practice the language to speak about Reiki with clarity and in uncompromising terms. This is a careful and thoughtful journey where instruction becomes knowledge.

To be clear, while a teacher can perform an attunement and make Reiki accessible to a student (level 1) and then teach them how to be a practitioner (level 2), a teacher can't make the student a Master beyond the title. The student must take the guidance and instruction of the teacher and through their own personal commitment and work, truly attain mastery.

The Master's course is taught over a two-day period and, like levels 1 and 2, includes classroom instruction, an attunement ceremony, and practice. Unlike the earlier levels, however, I encourage my Master level students to also write articles about Reiki. They can come up with their own topic, and they do not have to publish the articles they write, but I do encourage writing as a means to gain greater understanding of their thoughts in regard to Reiki. I also encourage my Master level students to work as mentors for the level 1 students, and I encourage them to take part in case study courses. I make none of these extracurricular items a requirement, but it is encouraged to help the student get to a place where they truly feel like a Master. I also offer recaps of the course, like I do in level 2. Again, those classes do not include an attunement, and I offer these classes at a discount relative to the original course that includes the attunement.

Level 4 — Teacher

A teacher is a channel for the teachings of Reiki – this is not unlike a student becoming a channel for Reiki once attuned. It is a role dedicated to the service of teaching, mentoring and creating channels. Meaning: teachers will teach, mentor and attune. The teacher training level follows the Master level. A teacher starts as a Master but has expressed the interest and exercised the desire to learn how to teach others and perform attunement ceremonies. It is a unique specialization, which is why the Master level and the teacher level are best taught separately.

Mastery of any subject is separate from mastery in teaching or even competence in teaching, and this difference is best honored and respected. Teaching is a calling and not one that all Masters will receive. For this reason, no one should be pushed or pressured into teaching. At this level, the teacher's goal to is teach Masters how to teach and mentor others at all levels of attunement and how to perform the attunement rituals. To do this well, a teachers' training should take weeks, assuming it's taught during a weekly schedule or taught over a two-to-three-month period, if the courses are taught on weekends. My last teacher training was taught over the course of three weeks with four to five full days of instruction each week, and still, I wish I had more time with my students.

The levels of Reiki are condensed but complete. Moving from one to the other feels like a big leap because it is. Each level will provide insights that support the student in learning, changing and deepening their personal relationship to Reiki and to self-care as a whole. My hope is that you not only find this explanation helpful, but that it gently encourages to move through the levels of attunement that you feel personally called toward.

Closing Thoughts

Inspiration is often found at the end of a question. A question is asked, and it often begs those within listening distance to think about things differently. Sometimes, this type of inspiration is born from trying to help someone else understand something. Sometimes the inspiration is born from someone asking a question that shows you that they have thought about the subject in a way that is new to you, and that newness calls you forward and invites you to look at things differently. To me, a follow-up question in Reiki offers such inspiration.

Born from practice, a follow-up question is a mind trying to make sense of what the body or its energy field feels or has experienced. This makes a follow-up question the question of the active seeker, one who is already on the path, seeking additional navigation from a teacher. It is for this reason that these questions are best met with patience and reverence both from the teacher answering and from the eager student who has asked. Patience and reverence are especially helpful if the student needs to wait until the teacher can think through the question and deliver an answer worthy of it.

Lately, I've found that answering follow-up questions is the part of teaching I'm enjoying most at the moment, and that is because of the challenge they present and the potential for inspiration that they offer. To be sure, this book would not have been written without the students who dared to asked questions and in so doing, gently asked for more from me and from themselves. The questions my students have asked me over the years have inspired me to write, create curriculums for all levels of attunement and pushed me to further my own study and understanding of Reiki. May you continue to ask follow-up questions in Reiki and beyond, and at one point, may you challenge yourself to answer the follow-up questions of those who will follow you.

Now on to Part IV, our final section, and one that helps us better understand Reiki by better understanding its differences to other commonly used and practiced healing systems.

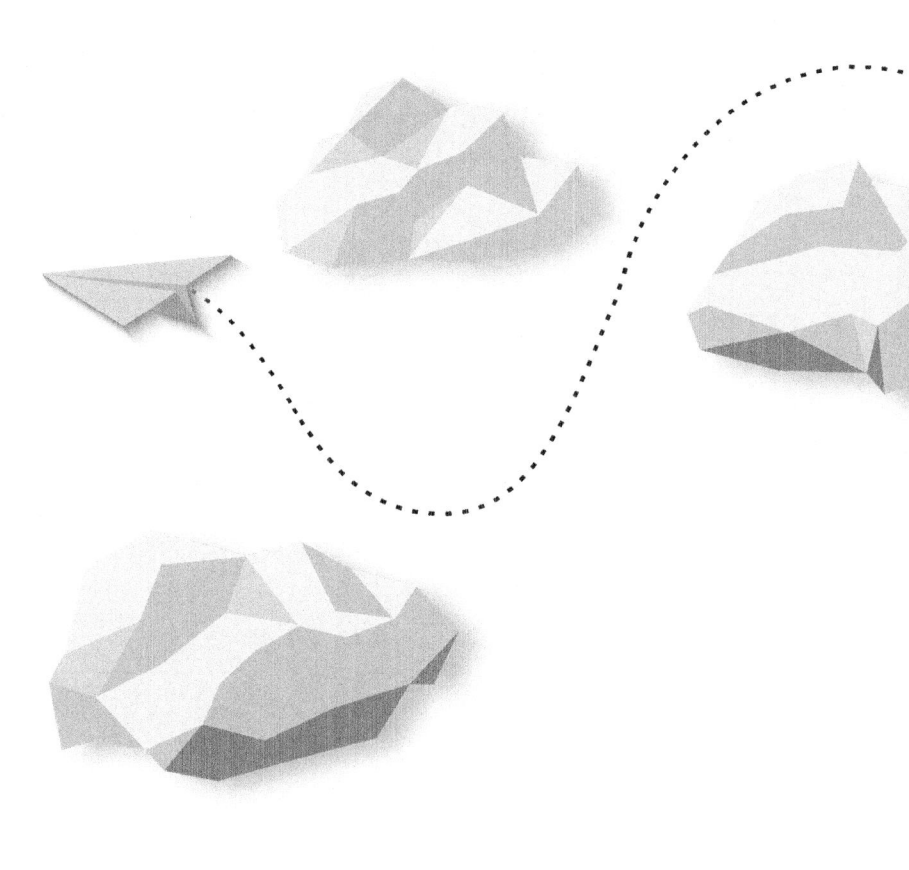

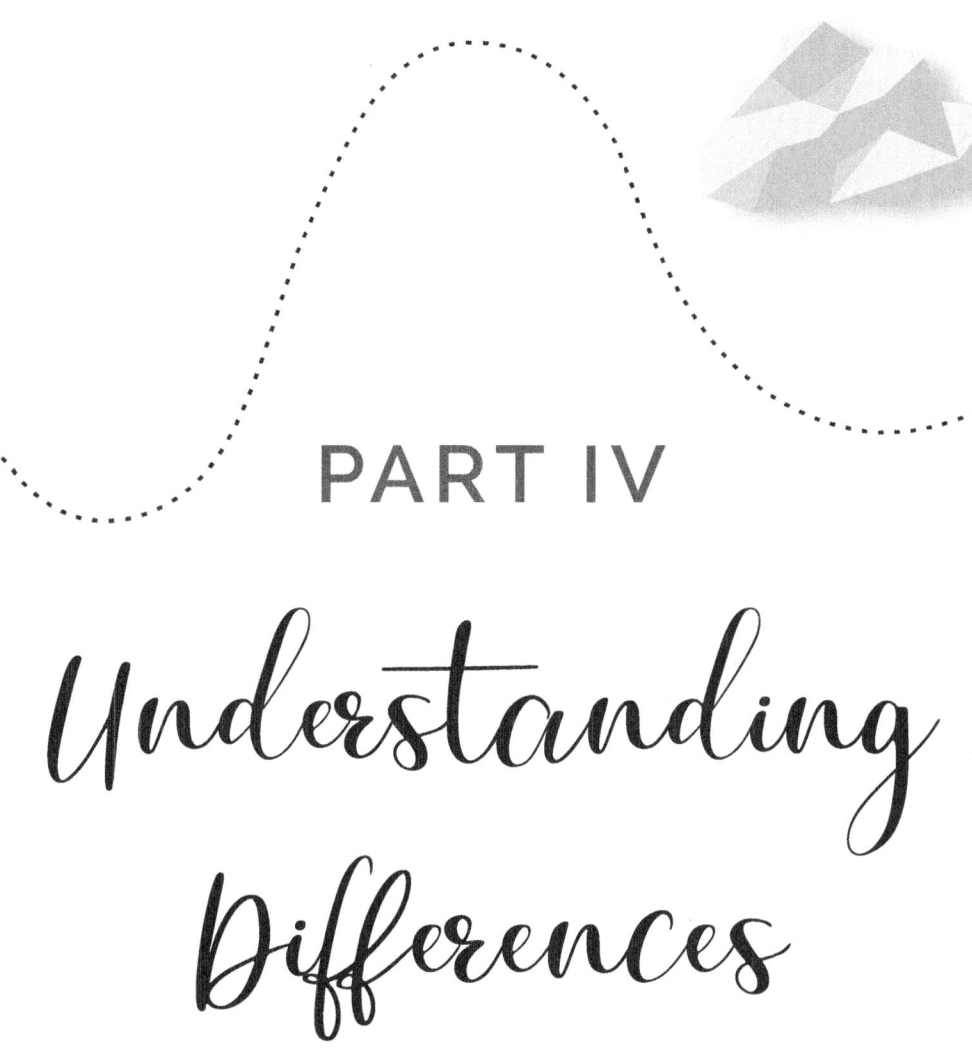

PART IV

Understanding Differences

Introduction

"Is Reiki like acupuncture?"
"Is Reiki like craniosacral therapy?"
"Is it like meditation?"
"I think I got Reiki once during a massage, is Reiki like massage?"
These are all good questions, and they're real questions I've received from students and from clients thinking about becoming students. These questions often follow up my initial explanation of Reiki and are asked in an effort to better understand Reiki by relating it to something they've either heard of or already tried. I also know these questions aren't only asked of teachers; my students get questions like this all the time when they talk to family and friends about Reiki. So, some time ago I started writing essays to help answer some of these questions.

The world of natural healing is fairly vast, but it's also tribal and secretive, which means its language is often vague, and healing methods are often lumped together under the umbrella of alternative or complementary care. People think choosing one is like choosing from a menu, and you just pick the one that sounds good to you at the time to see if it helps. But I think as a community, we can do better than that. We can instead provide clear guidelines on what our key practices are so that we can help people choose a healing method based on what it does and what it offers, and how likely that method is to help with a particular problem. In this approach, people become more aware of how to best care for themselves, but they also gain an understanding of what the greater world of healing has to offer.

By understanding differences, we give ourselves a greater understanding of what it means to be well, what tools are available to us to use, and when its best to try a new method or seek an alternative or complementary method, particularly to help us with any symptom that persists when our go-to method isn't doing the trick. To be clear, each one of these methods works, and they will positively affect change, but that does not mean that any one of them can alleviate every symptom you have. In the same way that brushing your teeth will not cure your earache, you don't give up on brushing; you look for a remedy that addresses the inflammation in your ear, knowing without criticism or fault that it's not your toothpaste.

Please know these essays are not deep dives into any one of the healing methods included here. If you want to learn more about any of these, there are ample books and dedicated sites that will provide you with more detailed information. These essays are brief, direct and are focused on differentiating each of these healing methods from Reiki. Please note that I repeat in each essay what Reiki is instead of stating that once in a general place within the section. I do this intentionally, as some readers may want to see the difference in each essay instead of having to reference back to a single section while reading ahead.

> Acupuncture seeks to eliminate pain and dysfunction by improving the flow of energy through the body's meridian system.

> *Reiki provides the remedy and repair our physical body and aura need as a result of daily wear and tear.*

Understanding the Differences Between Acupuncture and Reiki

Acupuncture and Reiki are among the mostly widely known and accepted natural healing practices used in the world. Both practices place their origins and history in Asia, and both are considered by Western societies to be alternative, Eastern or complementary healing practices. Acupuncture and Reiki are both natural energy healing practices that are used to repair, remedy and replenish the energy system of the person receiving treatment. However, Reiki and Acupuncture accomplish this in different ways, by working on different energy systems and using different energy vibrations.

The human energy system runs through the physical body and surrounds it. Similar to the internal workings of our bodies, our energy system is comprised of complex systems that while separate, are inter-related and work together. While many have heard of and have a cursory understanding of the body's circulatory system, endocrine system and lymphatic system, few have heard of the different energy systems of the human body, which among other things includes a meridian system, an aura, a chakra system and an astral body. Despite this, our general health and well-being is determined by the health and functioning of each.

Acupuncture

Acupuncture seeks to eliminate pain and dysfunction by improving the flow of energy through the body's meridian system. It does this through the strategic and purposeful application of specialized needles through the skin on areas known as meridian points. This is done for the purpose of eliminating energy blockages within the meridian system. The energy that flows through the meridian system is qi (pronounced chi).

Qi is a vital energy that sustains life. It runs through the body and is available in nature and found throughout the planet. Blockages in the meridian system impede the flow of qi that runs through the body. Having a strong, unimpeded flow of qi mirrors health, and having a low, impeded flow of qi is when illness or injury is present. The practice of acupuncture is to restore proper flow and balance of qi. Blockages and imbalances left without remedy or treatment will result in injury, illness and a decreased capacity to engage in and enjoy daily activities.

Blockages have many causes. A block can be the result of trauma, injury, stress, emotional imbalance and poor lifestyle choices, such as bad diet and inactivity, to name a few. These blockages can be responsible for a host of symptoms and conditions, and when this is the case, acupuncture can be an effective treatment. To be clear, everyone has blockages from time to time. It's unavoidable and a part of life, but they can be remedied, and acupuncture is one of the courses of treatment for it. Reiki does not do any of these things mentioned above.

It takes years of study to become an acupuncturist, and many acupuncturists hold advanced college degrees. For this reason, acupuncture is considered a professional, advanced care treatment, similar to a dentist, psychologist or doctor.

Acupuncture is usually performed in a tranquil treatment room where the client lies on a table fully or partially clothed and comfortable. The acupuncturist identifies and places needles on the specific meridian points the client needs and then leaves the room, leaving the client in peace and the needles to do their work. Generally speaking, acupuncture is not painful. The needles do not need to go very deep.

Appointments need to be scheduled for an acupuncture session, and the approximate time for treatment is about forty-five minutes to an hour. Clients can expect to leave an appointment feeling relaxed, balanced and rejuvenated.

Reiki

Reiki seeks to provide the remedy and repair our physical body and the aura need as a result of wear and tear. The practice of Reiki involves the application of cupped Reiki hands applied directly on the body, or just above the person receiving Reiki. Reiki repairs and provides remedy to imbalances resulting from the wear and tear of daily life. These imbalances, if left untreated, will also result in physical ailments that include illness, injury and diminished capacity for and enjoyment of daily activities. This is a wear and tear that no one is immune from, because these imbalances are the result of living, doing, being. Everyone, each day has what we call wear and tear. Generally, we experience wear and tear as tension. Common symptoms include difficulty sleeping, emotional swings, lack of energy, and feeling like you have the inability to relax.

Because Reiki provides repair and remedy to daily wear and tear, it is ideal to receive Reiki every day. In this way, it can be helpful to compare Reiki and the need for it to hydration. In every moment of every day, your body is losing water. It's just a part of life itself. To adjust for that, we drink water in an attempt to restore what we lose each day. The need for Reiki is like that. It's the bit of energy self-care we need daily to keep us (in a sense) energy hydrated.

Reiki is more immediately accessible than Acupuncture. The barrier of entry to Reiki is extraordinarily low. Anyone can learn Reiki, and everyone is encouraged to. Reiki can be given by anyone that has received a Reiki attunement, and to attend a Reiki class takes just a few hours. Once you've had an attunement, you have become a channel for Reiki, and Reiki will flow from your cupped hand. Reiki can be given to others and/or used exclusively as a daily self-care practice. There is no licensure in Reiki, but you can join any one of a number of Reiki associations that offer directory inclusion and other Reiki-related benefits.

Reiki can be done throughout the day and even during other activities. For example, you can give yourself Reiki while in a meeting by simply placing your cupped Reiki hand on your lap, or while standing in line at the grocery store. Reiki can be something you give yourself, but it is also a healing treatment that can be given by a Reiki professional. Those sessions are generally made by appointment where the client lies down fully clothed and a practitioner gives the client Reiki. Appointments generally last forty-five minutes to an hour and clients can expect to leave relaxed, very relaxed. They can also expect to feel balanced and energized.

Distinctions

Acupuncture focuses mainly on the meridian system. The meridian system is an energy system that runs through the body. Acupuncture works with qi. Reiki provides remedy and repair to the physical body and the aura. The aura is the energy field that surrounds the body.

Reiki is the energy that is used in Reiki. Remember, Reiki is both the name of the healing vibration and the formal healing practice. Some people think that qi and Reiki are the same energy. They are not. If I were to compare these natural healing vibrations to physically tangible things, I would compare our need for qi to be equal to blood and our need for Reiki to water. Acupuncture is one method of working with qi and the meridian system, however it is not the only method. Acupressure, qi gong and tai chi are examples of practices that also work to balance and strengthen the flow of qi.

To my knowledge, Reiki is the singular practice for giving yourself Reiki. Once attuned, you will receive a small amount of Reiki just walking around, but it's not enough for what's needed daily. That is why practice is necessary.

To be clear, these two healing practices complement each other — they can't be considered substitutes for one another.

If you are using Reiki each day and still have a particular symptom, that means the cause for the symptom is not the result of daily wear and tear. The same holds true for acupuncture. If you are seeing an acupuncturist and a particular symptom is still bothering you, that means the cause of that symptom is not the result of an imbalance or impingement in your meridian system. Both healing practices are still working for you, and you're still receiving all the benefits they have to offer. So don't worry if a symptom isn't treated using one of these: keep looking, there are more healing practices to try.

We'll continue our journey into understanding these other healing practices and what makes them different to Reiki.

> *Meditation is a healing practice that promotes balance between body and mind.*

> Reiki provides the remedy and repair our physical body and aura need as a result of daily wear and tear.

Differences Between Meditation and Reiki

Meditation is so ubiquitous that you can find it in one form or another in almost every tradition across the globe. There are many different techniques and ways to meditate, but despite the variety in methods offered, the goal of meditation is always the same. Both the practices of meditation and Reiki are part of a good energy self-care regime, meaning that these are practices you can learn to do at home by yourself.

Reiki and meditation are both considered to be good practices for relaxation, and for this reason, people often confuse the two as interchangeable, or misunderstand them as being substitutes for one another. This is not the case. While both seek to provide balance and relaxation to those who practice, each accomplish this in different ways by focusing on different areas of the body.

Meditation

Meditation is a healing practice that promotes balance between body and mind. The goal of meditation is to get both the body and mind moving together at the same speed, so to speak. When this happens, a person experiences mental and emotional balance, as well as natural relaxation. To be clear, meditation does not use an external energy vibration to affect positive change. Instead, it's a practice that engenders more favorable brainwave activity through the careful regulation and self-management of what is commonly referred to as the "monkey mind" and bringing it into balance with the rest of the body. This means that meditation is an internal process where change occurs solely from within. Even when an outside stimulus is used for support, like music or a guided meditation, the change itself comes from internal processes and not from a change made through an external energy source.

The monkey mind is shorthand for describing a mind that is always going, one that's full of thoughts and never appears to take a rest. When the mind is overactive, it is out of sync with the rhythms of the rest of the body. This imbalance can cause many problems, but the common ones are stress and anxiety. The goal of meditation is to retrain the mind or create better habits for the mind that encourage it to slow down naturally and sync up with the rest of the body. This sync-up between body and mind is balance, and this balance engenders natural relaxation. When this happens, a person experiences what is commonly referred to as inner peace. The practice of meditation is a training for the mind and an intentional reprieve from a world that is constantly pushing it to go faster and overthink everything.

There are many different ways to practice meditation. You can take a class, join a seminar, or practice at home with a group or alone. Meditation is often incorporated into different types of classes, like yoga, and most classes on metaphysical subjects or gatherings of spiritual groups. You can meditate for hours or for minutes. You can meditate standing, sitting, walking or laying down. Generally speaking, meditation requires time set aside for practice and mental focus. The best style of meditation is the style that works best for you.

Reiki

The name Reiki refers to two separate but related things. Reiki is the name of the natural, external healing vibration that is used to create positive change, and it is also the name given to formal practice that teaches people how to use it. Reiki is a healing practice that promotes well-being, and it does this by providing remedy and repair to the physical body and the aura that is needed as a result of daily wear and tear. Daily wear and tear are the results of use and being — basically, it's the cost of being alive and having a body.

Reiki is necessary in a similar way that water is. Through living in your body, you are constantly using water and having to replenish what you use. Applying the concept of wear and tear to this example, dehydration would be considered wear and tear, and consuming water each day to replenish what your body uses would be its remedy. Reiki can be thought as the energy equivalent to that.

Once attuned, Reiki can be practiced throughout the day by placing your cupped Reiki hand on or above the body. Because it does not require mental focus, Reiki can be done alongside other activities and is relatively inconspicuous, meaning no one is likely to even notice if you're giving yourself Reiki while standing in the elevator.

Distinctions

To be sure, both practices are extremely valuable and worthy of time and practice. Where they intersect is that both yield a greater sense of balance and relaxation, albeit in different ways. Reiki is a preventive healing practice, and meditation, while also preventative, is more of a responsive healing practice. Meaning, meditation is more designed to provide remedy to a pervasive chronic condition (monkey mind) than to prevent the possibility of a condition due to unremedied wear and tear, like Reiki does.

While some people have called Reiki meditation, Reiki is not a form of meditation. It does not work on the mind and it doesn't seek to create change from within or bring internal processes into balance. Equally, meditation is not a healing practice that utilizes an external energy vibration to affect positive change. Meaning, it does not bring in something outside of the body to support, nourish or heal itself. The positive change meditation creates comes from within through dedicated practice.

If you currently practice both or are thinking of practicing both, and you already have a Reiki attunement, I have a fun exercise for you to try. Give yourself Reiki for five minutes and then meditate for ten minutes. No more — just that.

In classes that I've taught, students remark that using Reiki beforehand makes going into meditation easier. And there's an energy explanation for that. It's easier because in a manner of speaking, Reiki helps to knock off some of the energy noise and depletion that makes it just a bit harder to settle when you first sit down. This makes entering meditation a bit easier. This exercise has a dual purpose, though, and the second reason I suggest it is to show that these two practices are not substitutes but truly complements to one another. May they both become tools in your daily self-care toolbox if they aren't already.

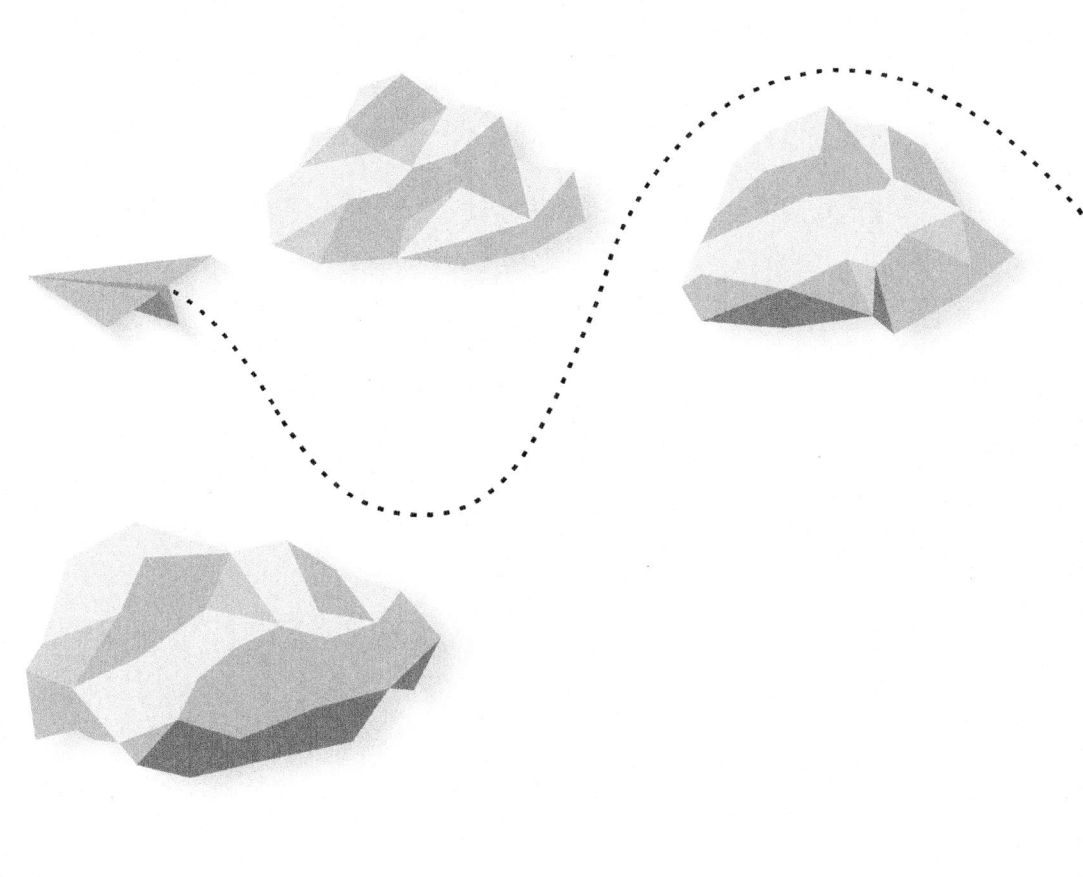

> Craniosacral therapy is a gentle, hands-on healing technique that seeks to release tension and pressure in an effort to restore function where dysfunction was once present. It does this through gentle adjustments of the bones in the skull, spine, pelvis and soft tissue release.

> *Reiki provides the remedy and repair our physical body and aura need as a result of daily wear and tear.*

The Differences Between Craniosacral Therapy (CST) and Reiki

There is no intersection between CST and Reiki other than the fact that both fall under the complementary care umbrella. CST is an offshoot of osteopathic medicine, and Reiki is a practice of energy medicine. Reiki is a preventative care practice, and CST is considered both a preventative and a reactive care practice, the latter meaning that it is seeking to provide relief from or cure to an existing condition. Generally, these two healing practices are not confused for one another, rather they are sometimes use in comparison in an effort to try to understand one by being compared to or likened to the other.

Craniosacral Therapy

CST is a gentle, hands-on healing technique that seeks to release tension and pressure in an effort to restore function where dysfunction was once present. CST practitioners are taught that by gently adjusting the bones of the skull, spine, pelvis and by releasing restrictions in the soft tissues, cerebrospinal fluid can be normalized and move without restriction, thereby improving the central nervous system and the body's ability to heal. CST does not use an external healing vibration to affect positive change. It uses touch and intuition to do that. Touch is used by applying gentle pressures around the skull and pelvic bones and in tissues along the spines. Intuition is used by CST practitioners to identify spots where pressure is believed to be and where touch is required.

CST practitioners complete a minimum of 100 hours of study, and some are also osteopaths, chiropractors and massage therapists. For this reason, CST, like acupuncture, is considered a professional, advanced care treatment, meaning you can't do this at home. CST is usually performed in a tranquil treatment room where the client provides information about the issue or issues they are experiencing and then lies on a table fully clothed while the practitioner makes gentle adjustments and releases areas where there was once compression. CST sessions generally last one hour.

Reiki

Reiki is a healing practice that promotes well-being by providing remedy and repair to the physical body and the aura that is needed as a result of daily wear and tear. Daily wear and tear are the results of use and being. Meaning, Reiki is meant to keep small imbalances small so that imbalances never reach the tipping point that takes it from imbalance to illness or injury.

It is similar to at-home oral hygiene in this way. A good daily at-home oral hygiene routine won't save you from the daily imbalances your mouth will experience throughout the day, because you have to eat and drink. But a dedicated practice will save you from having those small imbalances turn into problems that see you ending up in the dentist's chair with a problem that requires her drill — I hate that drill.

Reiki is primarily a self-care practice, but it is also an advanced care practice, meaning that you can see a professional for a session. Reiki provides remedy and repair by channeling the energy vibration, also aptly named Reiki. This means Reiki, the formal practice, is the application of the Reiki vibration channeled through a person and given to another or given to the self.

To practice Reiki you need an attunement, which means you need to attend a class with a Reiki teacher to both be attuned and learn how to use it. A level 1 Reiki class is usually taught in about four to six hours on a single day. Once attuned, Reiki can be practiced throughout the day, every day. Reiki can also be provided by a Reiki practitioner in a session. Like CST, Reiki sessions are commonly performed in a tranquil treatment room and last about forty-five minutes to an hour.

Distinctions

Reiki does none of the things that CST does, and equally CST does none of the things that Reiki does. Both seek to provide positive change but do so using different methods and with different goals in mind. The goal of CST is to alleviate compression so that cerebrospinal fluid can move throughout our spinal column smoothly, soothing pain, eliminating dysfunction and boosting our immune response. The goal of Reiki is eliminating symptoms of discomfort and unrest that are the result of daily wear and tear.

These two therapies can be used to complement each other, but they are clearly not adequate replacements for each other — even if the result of each session leaves you feeling relaxed and refreshed. To that end, if you are using one and wish to try the other, please consider trying it in addition to and not as a swap for. That way, you can ensure that you'll get the benefits of both without any sacrifice.

> *Massage is the pressing and/or rubbing of muscles, tendons and ligaments throughout the body.*

> Reiki provides the remedy and repair our physical body and aura need as a result of daily wear and tear.

The Differences Between Massage and Reiki

Massage is a very popular healing practice. In fact, it's likely the most popular healing practice and the one most regularly practiced. I posit that it was the first form of natural healing. Even today, it's the first type of healing children learn from adults who gently and carefully rub boo-boos and sore muscles as a means to relive pain and discomfort. Massage does not only ease pain and soreness, it provides comfort and communicates care. Like meditation, massage is known by and can be found in every culture around the world. There are countless techniques taught and methods used, but at its core, massage is something so natural to our humanity, it feels a part of our very nature and even a way we communicate love.

Massage and Reiki are often thought to be the same or similar things, and there's a reason for that. A fair number of massage therapists are also Reiki practitioners, many of whom offer both services and, in some instances, have developed a session that includes both. I have, on more than one occasion, had a new client tell me that they are not sure if they've had Reiki before but think they may have it one time in a massage. My heart always sinks a little when I hear that because they genuinely don't know if they've ever had Reiki before, and that always makes me a little sad, but then we quickly move to fix that.

Massage

Massage is the pressing and/or rubbing of muscles, tendons and ligaments. Massage can be done using the hand or using an instrument. A massage can be given with light, medium or hard pressure. The goal of massage is to release tension or spasm and to improve the flow of blood and lymphatic fluid throughout the body. Its sole focus is on the physical body and to deliver healing to it through firm, steady, rhythmic touch. Massage is credited with providing relaxation, naturally boosting immune response and improving circulation. Massage uses the body to heal the body. It does not use anything else external to it to affect positive change — massage oil in this instance does not count.

Massage is something that can be given to yourself or given to you informally at home by a friend or partner. Massage can also be something you receive professionally from a licensed massage therapist. A licensed massage therapist is generally trained in anatomy, physiology and kinesiology as well as in a variety of massage therapies and techniques. In addition to businesses that focus solely on massage, massage services can often be found at spas and chiropractic offices. Sessions are generally given in a tranquil treatment room where soft, relaxing music is played. Massages are generally given on a massage table and the person receiving the massage is often asked to disrobe themselves and lie under a sheet. A session generally lasts about an hour, and unlike most other professional physical and/or energy sessions, in some cultures it is customary to tip your massage therapist following the session.

Reiki

Reiki is a natural energy healing practice. It uses a subtle energy vibration named Reiki to deliver healing to the self or another. The way that vibration is delivered is through a formalized practice, also named Reiki. To be able to channel the vibration, a person needs to be attuned to it. Once attuned, the student learns how to use it. Reiki is practiced by using a specific hand position that, once engaged, enables Reiki to flow from it into the body. Reiki can include touch if the cupped Reiki hand is laid directly on the body, but it doesn't have to. You can also hold a cupped Reiki hand gently above the body as well.

Reiki promotes well-being by providing the remedy and repair we require as a result of daily wear and tear. Daily wear and tear are the result of use — not misuse or abuse, simply use. Use, and being. Wear and tear are the price we pay for living in a body. And it happens even when we're living gently and taking good care of ourselves. Wear and tear are unavoidable, but there is remedy to it, and that's Reiki.

Reiki is primarily a daily self-care practice, but it is also an advanced care practice, meaning that you can see a professional for a session. Reiki sessions are commonly performed in a tranquil treatment room and are scheduled by appointment. Clients lie down fully clothed on a massage table, and a Reiki professional gives the client Reiki. Appointments generally last about forty-five minutes to an hour.

Reiki and massage are similar in that they are both preventative and restorative healing practices that promote wellness and provide relaxation. And both are daily self-care practices that can be practiced each day, even if most people don't consider themselves as their own personal massage therapist. Despite this, however, I'm sure most people, on most days, do massage some part of themselves as a means to relieve pressure or reduce pain. Maybe it's a quick rub of the bottom of the feet or a momentary massage of the shoulder — it's all self-care. However, this is where the similarities between the two ends.

Distinctions

Massage uses the body to heal itself or another, and Reiki utilizes an external, natural energy vibration to provide healing. The focus of massage is on the physical condition of the body and in releasing tension and pressure within it. The focus of Reiki is providing remedy and repair to the subtler, energetic damage the body and the aura experience each day. Massage requires touch; Reiki can include touch but does not require it. Massage can be delivered using the hands or other smooth instruments, such as hot stones or bamboo. Reiki can only be delivered by a cupped Reiki hand. The cupped Reiki hand position is what, in a sense, turns Reiki on, and there is no substitute for it. This means that you cannot receive Reiki through massage, and you can't receive massage through Reiki. The hand requirements for each make that unworkable.

A massage therapist who is also attuned and trained to provide Reiki can offer a session that includes both Reiki and massage, but to be effective, each must be delivered separately during the session. To be sure, both Reiki and massage are enjoyable treatments to receive, and you are encouraged to use both regularly if not daily. These are healing practices that complement each other very well, but because they offer different benefits that are essential for wellness, they cannot be considered substitutes for one another.

Closing Thoughts

Understanding the differences between healing practices can help us understand not only the individual practices we examine but also what their place is in the larger world of natural healing. Often, we speak of these healing practices in a vacuum, and when we do include others in the conversation, it is generally to promote one service over another, unintentionally placing them in competition. This, however, limits our understanding of what options are available to us on the menu of wellness. Each practice will have its benefits, but that should not suggest that most are an adequate substitute for another, because even when the benefits appear to be similar, they may be the result of different work being performed on a different part of us. By understanding what different healing practices offer, in place of being in competition with one another, we become more empowered in our decision-making. We make our choices with discernment instead of feeling like it's part of a crapshoot.

Additionally, all our symptoms can help us choose which treatments are best for us, but this is best understood when we are maintaining our self-care practices, because when we are consistently practicing self-care, we can narrow the consideration set of causes. For example, if you're using Reiki every day but still having headaches, you can be fairly certain that your headaches are being caused by something other than wear and tear. This information goes a long way in helping a person determine that more is needed.

What also can be interesting to understand is that not all natural healing practices use energy to affect change. Some use the body, while others use internal processes like focus to effect changes from within. This understanding helps us broaden our view of natural healing and empowers us with information with which we can heal ourselves, even if healing ourselves means seeing a healing professional for a particular service.

So, I encourage you all to take a look at the menu, explore it and enjoy. What I have included here are a few of the items on that menu, but there are more to discover, and the power to do so is yours.

Author's Final Note

When I started this book, it was meant to be a compilation of articles I'd written about Reiki. At the time, I thought it would be a rather straightforward project, but the compilation I thought I was creating never quite came together. I worked and reworked it, but it wouldn't jell together, so in time I turned my attention to my students and to creating Reiki curriculums.

Strangely enough, I started off at level 2, but in hindsight it was the best place for me to start because it presented me with the challenge of bringing clear language to the level of Reiki that is quite arguably the hardest to teach. I later moved on to level 1, and in about a year or two to the Master level, and an easy two years after that, to the Teacher level. Each taught me new things about Reiki and myself, and in time I came to see that this book was never truly meant to be a compilation. It was meant to be a blueprint of how to think about Reiki if longevity of practice is the goal.

The principles found in this book lay the foundation for my curriculums. While my curriculums go into more detail and offer more tangents of discussion, the core messaging that fills the pages of this book are found in each level. To be sure, at the end of every course I taught, I found myself wishing I had a book I could give my students to support them after class ends. This book is for them, for it was their hopeful expressions, moments of wonder, and ah-ha moments that kept me coming back to this book, determined to complete it and determined to share it. I want to share it with them, but also with all Reiki students, because every student is in some way a seeker. This book is my effort to carefully place road signs along the seeker's journey. This book has easily been years in the making. It's also been a labor of love, and now that it's complete, I feel very proud of it. It's been a part of me for so long, and now it's been set free where I believe it can do the most good. I sincerely hope you enjoy it, and that it's helped make Reiki a part of your daily routine.

Thank You

To Dr. Karen Janes, who gently asked if I'd written another book yet. Her question and the hope with which she asked it, spurred the initial idea and inspiration for this book.

To Dr. Tiffany Hunter, who is always encouraging me to write and teach. Her dedication to helping me see this book to its final form was invaluable. She's been my editor, my sounding board and all-in-one focus group. She has made this a better book and me a better writer.

To Reggie Hunter, who has spent the length of our friendship supporting me and finding new ways to encourage and cheer me on. He worked very hard to take things off my plate so I could write and finish this book.

To Amelia Beamer, who if it were in her power would stop moving traffic, negotiate with a hurricane and delay the zombie apocalypse if it would give me time to write or teach. And in one way or another, she's managed to do all three.

To Kelly Cheetham Enriquez, Jeanette Riesgo Basto and Matt Kennedy, who have always believed in me, encouraged me and trusted me. In doing so, each gave me the courage to grow and helped me learn how to trust myself. These are lifelong, lifesaving, life-affirming friends and an extraordinary one-of-a-kind brother.

To my students, who through their excitement for learning have given me opportunities to learn more myself.

To Maya and Liam, who give hugs that say more than most words can aspire to, and whose eyes ask questions not yet realized but often leave me feeling deeply optimistic for what will come.

And as always, to my husband and teacher Jim Honey, who makes everything possible.

About the Author

Chyna Honey works and teaches at Healing for People in Marin County, California. In addition to the work she does as a healer and teacher of natural healing, she is also a restauranteur (Café del Soul), mother of two, wife to one and friend to many. She loves her work, really enjoys teaching and finds writing a real challenge, but for that reason, she also finds it incredibly rewarding. Her teaching and her writing are driven by a desire to help others understand healing and what it means to be well. She lives in Marin County, California with her family, and when she can, she travels long distances to see her much loved and admired friends and family. Chyna is also the author of *Understanding Reiki: from Self-Care to Energy Medicine*.

Printed in Great Britain
by Amazon